YOU ARE TEARING ME APART, LISA!

THE YEAR'S WORK:

STUDIES IN FAN CULTURE AND CULTURAL THEORY

Edward P. Dallis-Comentale and Aaron Jaffe, series editors

YOU ARE TEARING ME APART, LISA!

THE YEAR'S WORK ON *THE ROOM*, THE WORST MOVIE EVER MADE

EDITED BY ADAM M. ROSEN

INDIANA UNIVERSITY PRESS

This book is a publication of

Indiana University Press
Office of Scholarly Publishing
Herman B Wells Library 350
1320 East 10th Street
Bloomington, Indiana 47405 USA

iupress.org

 The paper used in this publication meets the minimum requirements of the American National Standard for Information Sciences—Permanence of Paper for Printed Library Materials, ANSI Z39.48–1992.

Manufactured in the United States of America

First printing 2022

Library of Congress
Cataloging-in-Publication Data

Names: Rosen, Adam M., editor.
Title: You are tearing me apart, Lisa! : the year's work on The room, the worst movie ever made / edited by Adam M. Rosen.
Description: Bloomington, Indiana : Indiana University Press, [2022] | Series: The year's work: studies in fan culture and cultural theory | Includes bibliographical references and index.
Identifiers: LCCN 2022003056 (print) | LCCN 2022003057 (ebook) | ISBN 9780253062710 (hardback) | ISBN 9780253062727 (paperback) | ISBN 9780253062734 (ebook)
Subjects: LCSH: Room (Motion picture) | LCGFT: Film criticism.
Classification: LCC PN1997.R57565 Y68 2022 (print) | LCC PN1997.R57565 (ebook) | DDC 791.43/72—dc23/eng/20220314
LC record available at https://lccn.loc.gov/2022003056
LC ebook record available at https://lccn.loc.gov/2022003057

To Lizzie, Benjamin, and Gabriel—you tear me apart.

Where there is no vision, the people perish.

—*Proverbs 29:18*

How could this happen? We started out like Romeo and Juliet but it ended up in tragedy.

—*Milhouse Van Houten*

CONTENTS

ACKNOWLEDGMENTS

Deepest appreciation first and foremost goes to all of the wonderful contributors to this book: Nathan Abrams, Lenika Cruz, James Curnow, John Donegan, John Dyck, Matt Foy, Keith Kahn-Harris, Amanda Ann Klein, James MacDowell, Ernest Mathijs, Renee Middlemost, Ross Morin, Landon Palmer, Hario Priambodho, Carter Soles, and Ellen Wright. You have greatly furthered the world's knowledge of *The Room,* and posterity will thank you. Many thanks as well to Tommy Wiseau for bestowing on the world your beautiful dark twisted fantasy. Shout-out to Dan Janjigian for the fantastic art and quick approval. Thank you, Margot Kahn and Laura Portwood-Stacer, for advice on anthology wrangling. Props to Ian Brereton for getting me hooked on *The Room* from Los Angeles and to Zach Saginaw, Matt Wasserman, and Ari Alter for cultivating the habit in New York. To their eternal credit, Barbara Teszler, Scott Teplitzky, Aaron Dahlstrom, Mary Ellen Dendy, Angela Polidoro, and Devin Whitney have ensured I never go a week without seeing a new meme or Irish musical parody inspired by *The Room*. Thanks to Andy Paul, bad movie connoisseur and perhaps the world's foremost scholar of *They Live*. Gigantic thanks to Molly Pisani for your feedback and encouragement throughout this entire process, beginning with the proposal; I am indebted to you as a person, as a human being, as a friend. Additional thanks to IUP staff, including Allison Blair Chaplin, Sophia Hebert, Rachel Rosolina, Lesley Bolton, and Gary Dunham. Thanks to *The Year's Work* series editors Ed Dallis-Comentale and Aaron Jaffe for seeing the potential in a project dedicated to something that's supposed to be "the worst." And, of course, thanks to the contributors to *The Year's Work in Lebowski Studies*, the inspiration for this anthology; I hope I didn't rip you off too badly. Biggest thanks of all to my family for your support, especially Lizzie, who has (mostly) not yet reneged on your promise to watch *The Room* at least once a year. And Benjamin and Gabriel—I cannot wait to toss the football with you.

YOU ARE TEARING ME APART, LISA!

INTRODUCTION

LET'S TOSS THE BALL AROUND

ADAM M. ROSEN

"Do you understand life? *Do* you?" So half asks, half begs the character Johnny, the profoundly suffering protagonist of *The Room,* during a dramatic confrontation with his fiancée, Lisa. It's a serious question posed by a very serious man. In fact, this inquiry is arguably the key to unlocking the mysteries of the movie, of which there are famously many. To understand life is to comprehend the truth expressed by *The Room,* an artistic fever dream powered by lots of money, lots of delusion, and sheer force of will that came into being as a full-length feature film in 2003.

The exasperation in Johnny's voice reveals his despair that Lisa, and the rest of the world, does *not* seem to understand life—at least not in the way that Johnny and his creator and real-life inspiration, a mysterious long-haired man named Tommy Wiseau, do. If *The Room* is a revelation, as Wiseau insists, well, nobody is willing (or able) to receive Johnny's gospel.

On the face of it, the problem is simply one of communication. What Wiseau insists is a gritty portrayal of adult romance and friendship gone tragically wrong is completely unrecognizable to the vast majority of adult humans. His message was lost in transmission, rendered incomprehensible by decisions in casting, production, dialogue, music, set design, cinematography, and wardrobe that made perfect sense to him but seemingly nobody else. For his efforts, *The Room* has been hailed by commentators as "the worst movie of all time," "the *Citizen Kane* of bad movies" (by contributor Ross Morin in *Entertainment Weekly*[1]), and "a movie that prompts most of its viewers to ask for their money back," to offer just a few representative assessments.

When it was released in the spring of 2003, *The Room* should have died and been forgotten, yet another Hollywood dream that failed to materialize. It appeared in a single theater in a single city, Los Angeles, for all of two weeks—and only that long because Wiseau rented the theater himself.[2] Against a rumored budget of $6 million, it collected a whopping $1,800 at the box office during its practically undetectable run.[3]

What a difference a decade or two makes. Today, *The Room* is a bona fide cult phenomenon, and an increasingly mainstream one. In cities around the United States and the world, the movie is shown, often monthly, at screenings that rival *The Rocky Horror Picture Show* for levels of fan intensity and ritual-filled performance (well, before the COVID-19 pandemic). Celebrities such as Seth Rogen and Paul Rudd have plugged *The Room* during interviews, and Kristen Bell claims to have hosted screenings of the film at her house for friends.[4] YouTube, Reddit, and Twitter teem with hundreds of memes (see fig. 0.1), commentary riffs,[5] and video mash-ups of *The Room*, many professionally produced and some with millions of views.[6]

In 2013, *The Room* even inspired a best-selling and critically acclaimed memoir about its making, *The Disaster Artist: My Life inside* The Room*, the Greatest Bad Movie Ever Made*. The tell-all was written by Greg Sestero, a former underwear model turned actor and *The Room* costar, and veteran journalist (and serious study of *The Room*) Tom Bissell. The book did such a masterful job of depicting the surreal events surrounding *The Room*'s production that it inspired a movie of the same name, a major motion picture released in

0.1 Meme posted in the r/room subreddit in April 2021, after the announcement of an additional round of stimulus checks for qualified US households in response to the COVID-19 pandemic: https://www.reddit.com/r/theroom/comments/m3aifo/wheres_my_f_money/.

December 2017. Produced by and starring James Franco, *The Disaster Artist* received a rapturous welcome at Cannes and earned two Golden Globe nominations (scoring Franco the win for his lead role) and an Oscar nomination for Best Adapted Screenplay.

The Room's peculiar delights have not gone unnoticed by academe, either. Today, many film instructors and film studies professors, contributors to this book among them, use the film as a teaching tool, both to dissect the anatomy of this special sort of cult film and to show students what *not* to do during the filmmaking process. Since the late

0.2 Johnny listens to Lisa behind closed doors. © 2003 by Wiseau-Films. (Movie still from *The Room*.)

2000s, when *The Room*'s conquest of the underground began picking up steam, articles about the movie have been appearing in various film and media studies journals.

Slowly but surely, *The Room* has become *the* cult film of the current age. Surprisingly, though, until now there have been no books of criticism about this once-in-a-generation work of cinematic catastrophe. *You Are Tearing Me Apart, Lisa!: The Year's Work on* The Room, *the Worst Movie Ever Made* aims to remedy this unfortunate state of affairs.

In the following pages, you will encounter an ambitious collection of essays examining this remarkable cult sensation from many different angles. The collection draws from an accomplished group of writers in academia and journalism, all of whom are as astounded, appalled, and enchanted by *The Room* as I am (and, probably, you are). Some, as you will discover, are also conflicted about the movie's message and the reported conduct of its creator and have come to reconsider their interest in both. Whatever their perspective, each contributor brings clarity and context to what first appears to be an incomprehensible mess, revealing the timeless power of this uniquely terrible production, one of the most fascinating failures in film history.

The Room has been a pet obsession of mine ever since a friend sent me clips of its most infamous, cringeworthy scenes (and that's saying a lot, considering that the entire movie, from opening to closing credits, fits the technical definition of *cringeworthy*). That was in 2009, right around the time *The Room* had begun to attract attention outside the realm of film diehards and comedy nerds, when blogs were still the go-to place for tracking pop culture. My friend lived in Los Angeles, so he was more tapped into the film world, where *The Room*'s fandom first took hold. I still remember the very first clip I saw, posted on Videogum (RIP): a scene where Johnny (Wiseau) wails that Lisa is "tearing him apart!" in a shameless rip-off of James Dean in *Rebel Without a Cause*. I was horrified—and hooked. When it was announced a few months later that the movie would be making its New York debut at a theater in the East Village, I started rounding up friends to attend.

I soon discovered that *The Room* was all it was rumored to be—and much worse. Think of every trait of a successful or even merely forgettable film; whatever they are, *The Room* doesn't have them. Continuity is nonexistent. Multiple gratuitous sex scenes go on for full minutes. Characters and subplots appear and disappear as if by magic. The film looks like it was shot on a stage, even though it supposedly cost millions of dollars to make. And, most memorably for viewers, the dialogue ranges from utterly banal ("If a lot of people loved each other, the world would be a better place to live") to strange ("Keep your stupid comments in your pocket!") to downright nonsensical ("My Lisa's great when I can get it").

The film consumed me. Soon after the screening, I purchased a DVD directly from the Wiseau-Films website and proceeded to show it to ignorant friends and a few hapless romantic interests for years. I even arranged a screening of my own at a theater in Brooklyn that sold out. Each viewing revealed yet another layer of staggering incompetence or sheer weirdness.

But *The Room* is so much more than just a bad—nay, terrible—movie. Calling it "the worst movie ever made" isn't inaccurate, but the superlative sells the film woefully short. In truth, *The Room* is a priceless cultural artifact. Because even if by complete accident, it touches on so many topics of modern concern, including sincerity, authenticity, performance, artistic value, Americanness, Hollywood, and masculinity—hell, even life itself. Just as Johnny promises.

Though it stands at the top (bottom?) of the heap, *The Room* is hardly alone in its "badness." There's a long and illustrious canon of "bad" films and, thus, a spectrum of supposed crimes against cinema. On one end are technically or artistically challenged films like *Plan 9 from Outer Space*, *Troll 2*, *Birdemic*, and most of the works of the German restaurateur turned filmmaker Uwe Boll. Films like this stick out because of cinematography lapses, poor writing, or other conspicuous problems that reveal "the seams" of the film, "the mismatched and poorly executed fabrics of its construction," as contributor Amanda Ann Klein puts it. At the other end are professionally produced but simplistically earnest films like *Road House*. Its plot—a New York City bouncer is recruited to bring order to an unruly, organized-crime-infested bar in small-town Missouri—is ludicrous, to quote Maude Lebowski (incidentally, describing another notoriously bad film, *Logjammin'*). But *Road House* has a rocking blues soundtrack, immortally dumb quotes ("Pain don't hurt"), and perfectly cheesy performances by Patrick Swayze, Ben Gazzara, and Sam Elliott. It's certainly not *The Godfather*, but in its fun, unpretentious way, it's extremely entertaining. It's "bad" in that it's lowbrow or pandering—which may not necessarily make it "bad" at all. (More on this shortly.)

On closer inspection, much of what is commonly derided as "bad" turns out to be simply cheap, technically incompetent, unconventional, or in poor taste. To be sure, a lack of money isn't always correlated with a "worst" label; big-budget turkeys like *Showgirls*, *Battlefield Earth*, and *Gigli* had plenty of star power and studio money behind them. But many bad movies' flaws stem more from a lack of resources than irredeemable moviemaking. Ed Wood offers an illustrative example. The comically cheap-looking flying saucers in *Plan 9 from Outer Space*, so mocked over the years, were rumored to be toys purchased by the director. But the film itself, while delivered in robotically stilted dialogue, has a coherent sci-fi plot when it comes down to it. (Though the fact that it revolves around a corpse-resurrecting alien named Eros probably didn't help its reputation with late-1950s tastemakers.) In recent years, some critics have even come to revise their opinion of the filmmaker, lauding him for his forward-looking exploration of gender norms in *Glen or Glenda*—another supposed "bad film" firmly in the cult canon.[7]

Apart from money issues, many "bad" movies are dubbed as such because of an outlandish or distasteful premise. In *Birdemic*, well, there's an epidemic . . . of killer birds. *Gigli* revolves around a hit man who kidnaps a mentally disabled child while trying to turn his lesbian coconspirator straight (not exactly Ben Affleck's finest moment). Nevertheless, most of these films still have some sort of intelligible logic. Even *Birdemic* and *Troll 2* operate within a recognizable story arc.

But *The Room*, in all of its audacious ambition, had no outlandish premise. And it had plenty of money—that rumored $6 million. (For comparison, *Birdemic* was supposedly made on a budget of $10,000.) It wasn't going to wow its audience by blowing things up or killing people, pandering, or titillating viewers—the typical tricks of "bad" filmmakers. It was meant to be nothing more than a simple but authentic relationship drama, a new twist on a familiar story of love gone wrong. "You want to be fake? Not me. I hate fake stuff," Wiseau warned his crew during production.[8] An overly serious relationship drama, set mostly in the same interior location, made by a wealthy eccentric with complete control? Now that's the stuff of badness immortality.

In many ways, *The Room* represents a new era in cult cinema (which, it's worth mentioning, is distinct from "bad cinema," despite a high degree of overlap). For most of film history, audiences had to attend specially organized screenings, often late at night, to see a "cult" film (more accurately, a film retroactively bestowed with the label). The feeling of having to *work* to see a movie, to deliberately go out of your way to seek it out, often at odd times and odd places (many screenings of early John Waters films were held in Baltimore churches, a fact that still amazes and horrifies me), fostered a sense of shared experience that contributed to audience members' gratification. Physical participation and the sense of belonging it nurtured were, and arguably still are, as central to the experience as the actual movie itself. It's how screenings of *The Rocky Horror Picture Show* evolved from a showcase of camp silliness to full-on events with their own language, behaviors, code of conduct, and values.

In the mid-1990s, however, shifts in technology began to disrupt the typical cult movie discovery-and-adoption cycle. Critic Judy Berman dates a point of inflection to *The Blair Witch Project*, whose low-budget "guerrilla marketing" campaign (as the press at the time called it) "lured viewers to a website where they could investigate the supposedly true story of three student filmmakers who disappeared in the woods."[9] The internet, and user interactions with it, soon became a central part of the movie experience, both for mainstream entertainment consumers and for those inclined toward cult films. Around the same time, DVD players and high-resolution flat-screen TVs became increasingly affordable, prompting millions of Americans to spend movie night at home. And then came streaming.

Berman explains that "as the internet eclipsed the cinema as a point of convergence for cultists, DVD-by-mail startups, file-sharing services, and then streaming video platforms made it possible to consume even the most obscure movies without leaving home. If you wanted to see Todd Haynes's banned Barbie-doll musical *Superstar: The Karen Carpenter Story* in the nineties, you had to wait for an arthouse theater to schedule a secret screening. Now you can usually find it on YouTube."[10]

As *The Room* coursed its way through the underground in the mid and late 2000s, unlike with cult films of the past, many if not most early viewers were first exposed to it via home viewing parties or clips on the internet. Think of Kristen Bell or Paul Rudd, slapping their knees next to bowls of microwave popcorn. The raucous, *Rocky Horror Picture Show*–esque public screenings of *The Room* are obviously a huge part of its current identity and have been vital to its global spread. But while they certainly have increased *The Room*'s profile and molded legions of new fans, they were less crucial in creating the original interest in the film. Many of these public screenings were offered in response to the

0.3 The author (*right*) and fellow fan of *The Room* Zach Saginaw on Halloween 2010 in New York City. Courtesy of the author.

movie's existing, largely online infamy; in other words, the typical cult cycle was reversed.

Additionally, by the early 2000s advances in video recording technology made moviemaking much more accessible, allowing any amateur with enough money (but not necessarily that much) to make a feature-length film, a topic touched on in chapter 15. All of which is to say, the conditions were just right for *The Room* to claim its place in the pantheon of cinematic failure.

Of course, calling a movie bad is, in the end, a value judgment. One person's bad movie is another one's great or just OK movie. As chapter 4 explores in detail, calling something bad presumes there is a good it can be measured against, that there must be an objective way to classify a film, work of art or literature, or any other cultural product. It suggests that value is merely a matter of meeting certain criteria. But is this really true or tenable? If it is, the repercussions are unsettling—for those policing the criteria of what makes something good as much as for those who fail to live up to it.

You Are Tearing Me Apart, Lisa! is an attempt to grapple with this topic through its deep exploration of a single unforgettable work of art. Apart from investigating *The Room*'s various meanings, and what they tell us about the movie and the society that would allow such a work to be produced, this book seeks to help readers examine their assumptions and perhaps think a bit differently about art and, just maybe, even their own lives. Badness, after all, is an integral part of every one of us. Maybe, the critic Phil Christman suggests, in an imperfect world where hope for true connection is ultimately a fantasy, the real "bad movie" is our individual existence: "Just as everything you say can be misheard, or scrambled by differences in connotation or dialect, your presence in the world rarely says what you intend. You are a walking contradiction between aspiration and effect. The actual you orbits the intended you, the firm and defensible you, the serious you; or perhaps it's the other way around. This is a quality you share with me, and with everyone, and that makes all of us that desperate and self-deluded and wholly compelling phenomenon, the bad movie."[11]

The Room hasn't held up (as if it ever could have). In light of the #MeToo movement and recent reckonings with sexism in Hollywood and elsewhere, its undisguised chauvinism and flippant treatment of domestic abuse feel of a different age. And yet, as several contributors astutely point out, in its sexist message and alleged treatment of some female cast members, *The Room* is just like the slick professional production it aspired to be.

Such a film is likely to be considered problematic (to use the parlance of our times) by some today. Indeed, some viewers, including a few contributors, have made it clear that they are increasingly uncomfortable with the film, or at least laugh at it much less now that the abovementioned issues have come under stronger scrutiny. Has this harshed *The Room*'s bad-movie mellow? Should *The Room* be reconsidered—or even canceled? Well, that's a judgment call. The issue of whether problematic art can be valuable is considered by several commentators. I leave it up to you, the reader and viewer, to decide.

This book is divided into five sections. The first (Cliché and Convention, Misapplied) breaks down just what makes *The Room* so bad and what its many flaws can teach us about Hollywood and art. The second (Unlocking *The Room*) explores the messages and themes in the film, as well as its various cultural, cinematic, and literary influences. The third (Cult and the [Class]*Room*) offers edifying perspectives from instructors who use the film as a teaching tool, and the fourth (Fan Reception) focuses on *The Room*'s fan culture and unique cult values. The final section (Constructing Tommy Wiseau) reflects on the persona and legacy of the film's infamous writer, financier, star, director, and promoter.

Feel free to read the chapters in order or jump around as you like. Despite the section groupings, each essay is self-contained and can stand on its own. However you approach the collection, you'll leave with a new appreciation for just how good something so bad can be.

That's the idea, huh?

ADAM M. ROSEN is a nonfiction book editor and writer in Asheville, North Carolina, and a former associate editor in the Reference Division of Oxford University Press. He has contributed to the *Atlantic*.com, the *Los Angeles Review of Books*, the *Baltimore Sun*, the *Onion*, and many other print and online outlets.

Notes

1. See Collis, "Crazy Cult of *The Room*."

2. According to Sestero, a movie had to be shown in theaters for at least two weeks to be considered for an Academy Award.

3. Sestero and Bissell, *Disaster Artist*, xiv, 263.

4. Collis, "Crazy Cult of *The Room*."

5. Often just called a riff, this refers to a scene-by-scene commentary—typically on a "bad" film—that's usually comedic and often vulgar. YouTube features thousands of them, if not more. The art form was popularized by the cult TV show *Mystery Science Theater 3000* and is the main topic of chap. 11.

6. For some illustrative examples, see Gregory Brothers, "Songify *The Room* (You're Tearing Me Apart)," YouTube, December 1, 2017, https://www.youtube.com/watch?v=ttKn1eGKTew&t=148s; PistolShrimps, "*Star Wars* with Tommy Wiseau—Oh hi Mark," YouTube, May 5, 2017, https://www.youtube.com/watch?v=dXlao2KNYjQ&t=14s; Channel Awesome, "*The Room*—Nostalgia Critic," YouTube, July 14, 2010, https://www.youtube.com/watch?v=Tri9i3WtXLc&t=479s; Nick Lutsko, "*The Room* as a Prince Song (Extended Version)," YouTube, May 14, 2019, https://www.youtube.com/watch?v=F1ept4kyafE.

7. Craig, *Ed Wood, Mad Genius*, 68.

8. Sestero and Bissell, *Disaster Artist*, 251.

9. Berman, "Streaming Void."

10. Berman, "Streaming Void."

11. Christman, "Cinema of Inadvertence."

PART I
CLICHÉ AND CONVENTION, MISAPPLIED

CHRIS-R'S GUN 1

THE ROOM *AS AN UNCONSCIOUS PARODY OF HOLLYWOOD FILM CONVENTIONS*

CARTER SOLES

In one of the best scenes in *The Room*, drug dealer Chris-R (Dan Janjigian) pulls a gun on young Denny (Philip Haldiman), cornering the young man on the film's notorious rooftop set and shouting one of my personal favorite lines of the movie: "Where's my fucking money, Denny?!" (see fig. 1.1). This confrontation leads to at least two absurd and unresolved situations: First, in the one the film focuses on, Denny's surrogate mother and object of desire, Lisa (Juliette Danielle), interrogates him about the exact nature of his involvement with Chris-R, repeatedly asking him "what kind of money" he owes to Chris-R and what drugs he obtained from the angry dealer. As with so many dialogues in *The Room*, this one goes nowhere—Denny never really explains what happened, and his involvement with Chris-R is never mentioned again after this one impassioned scene.

The second unresolved element of Chris-R's confrontation with Denny and others concerns what happens to the drug dealer himself after this scene. He is disarmed and dragged from the rooftop by Johnny (Tommy Wiseau) and Mark (Greg Sestero), never to be seen, heard from, or mentioned again. While this may seem like a minor plot point, yet another dead end in a movie packed with them, this one has potentially major repercussions down the road: it invokes the specter of Chekhov's gun, a storytelling convention attributed to playwright Anton Chekhov whereby a prop or plot element introduced early on in

18 a narrative should play a significant role in some later, often climactic scene of that same tale.

This rule is not meant to be rigidly prescriptive—it is OK to introduce red herrings and thematic or mood-enhancing elements that serve no direct plot function—but it is generally considered good storytelling practice to pay off any major developments in some way. As Chekhov reportedly put it, if you make a big deal of showing a gun in the first act, then that gun had better go off in a later one. Yet, in defiance of this notion and as with so many of *The Room*'s plot developments, the question of Chris-R—and equally importantly, his gun—is never concretely answered. The film simply does not care about Chris-R or the drug-dealer plot before or after this single scene. The scene, character, and gun are cut completely loose from narrative causality or the usual conventions of setup and payoff proposed by Chekhov and relentlessly deployed by Hollywood. It is perfectly emblematic of the film's disregard for, and unwitting parody of, the conventions of Hollywood storytelling and filmmaking.

In his 2010 article about *The Room* for *Harper's Magazine*, "Cinema Crudité: The Mysterious Appeal of the Post-camp Cult Film," Tom Bissell writes that *The Room*'s writer/director/star/financier/producer Wiseau "understands the placement and required tone of certain [Hollywood] conventions but not at all their underlying meaning."[1] Indeed, a great many familiar Hollywood narrative and visual conventions are present in *The Room*, just strangely applied and misused at almost every conceivable turn.

Take, for example, the incredibly stupid phone-tapping plot, about which co-lead actor and line producer Greg Sestero writes, "The interesting thing about Mark and Lisa's phone-tapped conversation is that *The Room*'s audience hears the original conversation they have in real time, on-screen; however, when Johnny plays their conversation back a

1.1 Artistic rendering of Chris-R and Denny's rooftop meeting. Courtesy of Dan Janjigian.

few seconds later, the recording is different from what the audience just heard—and yes, that difference is actually in the script."[2]

As if that blatant, apparently intentional (or at least scripted) continuity error weren't enough to sink the scene's believability, there's more: *Johnny himself* listens at the door while Lisa talks to Mark over the phone. So he doesn't need the tape recording—he already knows what she says to him, or he at least has the gist of it. And surely he must have guessed by this late hour who the man on the other end of the line must be. After all, he had just come to blows with Mark over his public canoodling with Lisa at a party earlier the same night.

Or there's the scene in which Johnny enters his favorite flower shop early in the film and the clerk says she does not recognize him at first—as if it would be remotely possible to not recognize Wiseau, with his long black hair, vampirish looks, and "strikingly asymmetrical face," as Bissell describes it.

Actually, *The Room*'s unconscious satire of Hollywood film conventions begins right out of the gate, with its opening credits and first two scenes. The movie's first shot is a panoramic shot of blue sky that tilts down to reveal San Francisco's Golden Gate Bridge. Meanwhile, the overwrought score sounds like C. J. Vanston's corny, low-budget orchestrations for *Red, White, and Blaine,* the play within a film in *Waiting for Guffman,* or the theme music for a cheaply produced daytime soap opera, which *The Room* essentially is.

Minus the cheesy music, the film's opening-credits montage of San Francisco exteriors evokes, perhaps, Hitchcock's *Vertigo,* yet its music and titles suggest a low-budget, amateurish indie film even before a single line of Wiseau's otherworldly dialogue is uttered. And those credits: Wiseau's name is repeated numerous times, with separate credits for him as executive producer, writer, producer, and director. This is the film's first notable moment of clear (yet unintentional) parody, for such oddly repetitive credits evoke the joke credits seen in Monty Python or Mel Brooks films, calling attention to themselves in a way that's (in this case unwittingly) hilarious. They merely foreshadow the greater crimes against Hollywood's conventions yet to come.

Denny's first entrance solidifies the utter weirdness of what we're seeing—his expressed interest in watching Lisa and Johnny have sex makes us think the film might actually deliver on its *Vertigo*-esque opening imagery and develop into a creepy erotic thriller. Or perhaps a post–New Queer Cinema exploration of sexual fluidity. But no, it quickly veers into an unappealing, soft-core sex scene of the resolutely heterosexual kind. In fact, the Johnny-Lisa sex scene leans so hard into Hollywood sex-scene clichés—gauzy bed curtains, rose petals, and cascading water feature prominently displayed—that it instantly makes a mockery of such scenes. And it drags on and on, lacking chemistry and running uncomfortably long for a scene ostensibly located in a "serious" melodrama. Maybe one would expect sex to feel this squirmily uncomfortable near the end of a proper erotic thriller like *Fatal Attraction* or *Sea of Love*, but here it is difficult to know how to respond to it, except with laughter or mild disgust.

It should be noted that the tone of this scene, and its low-budget circa-1990s R & B music, is replicated in the later scenes of Lisa trysting with her illicit lover (and Johnny's best friend, lest we forget), Mark. These recurring elements lend those scenes equal weight and value to Lisa's sex scenes with Tommy, so although it is arguably more conceivable that Mark and Lisa might be attracted to each other, the film does not indicate which, if any, of the film's sexual encounters should really mean something to the viewer and which should be seen as immoral or dangerous. Neither love nor illicit passion is conveyed by any such scenes. They simply all feel the same—uncomfortable, drawn-out, clichéd, and corny.

It is especially odd that this is the kind of scene *The Room* leads off with—an extended sexual encounter between Johnny and Lisa. Or at least it is rendered odd by the way it is set up and executed. Johnny and Lisa's relationship is established entirely via woodenly articulated clichés: he buys her a slinky red dress, she goes upstairs to try it on for him, and she descends the stairs, feet in close-up like Barbara Stanwyck's in *Double Indemnity*, as Johnny says, "Wow, you look so sexy, Lisa!" from off-screen. Only, unlike in most Hollywood romance scenes, young neighbor Denny intervenes, coming into the condo in the middle of the couple's "sexy" talk, inexplicably eating a few bites from an apple, then following them upstairs to join them in a precoital pillow fight on their bed. The opening scene's tone careens from sensual to jokey to impossible to fathom: "Welcome to this bizarro world where nothing makes sense and you don't know what kind of movie you're watching and—here's a sex scene!" Given the lack of motivation the film gives us for really caring about Johnny or Lisa, I almost wish Denny *had* been allowed to get involved somehow, just to make this scene (and another one almost exactly like it later on) memorable for something other than longish takes of Johnny's upraised, undulating white ass.

But pointlessness seems to be the film's final takeaway. In his book *The Disaster Artist*, Sestero chooses Steven as his avatar for *The Room*'s parodic inversion of movie storytelling. Not sure who Steven is? You could be forgiven. The character suddenly appears for the first time at the party scene, standing aside Michelle as he tries to convince Lisa of her wrongdoing even though we have no idea who he is (see fig. 1.2). "Steven is *The Room* personified," Sestero writes, contending that the whole film is an expression of "Stevenness—in which things happen for no clear reason."[3] The truth is, one can choose any number of similar examples—Claudette's breast cancer, Denny's drug dealings, Chris-R's gun—as a microcosm of the absurd whole because *The Room* is nothing if not consistent in its adherence to the principles of inconsistency and incompetence. Its every bizarre move makes its viewer painfully aware of how many other Hollywood movies, even ostensibly "bad" ones, get this basic stuff generally right. It is the consistency, the relentlessness of *The Room*'s mistakes and gaffes that transforms the film into an unwitting send-up of the simplest conventions of plot and character that we so take for granted. *The Room* makes us notice (and laugh at) those things that typically remain (relatively) invisible. Its amateurish pointlessness reveals how artificially constructed "meaning" is in Hollywood cinema in general.

1.2 Michelle and Steven. © 2003 by Wiseau-Films. (Movie still from *The Room*.)

Perhaps *The Room* really wants to be that dark, erotic thriller potentially hinted at by its opening credits and its introduction of the weird sexual dynamics between Johnny, Lisa, and the voyeuristic youngster Denny. It surely sees Lisa as an ultimate femme fatale, soullessly manipulating the film's helpless male leads, corrupting Mark and driving Johnny to self-destruction. As they sit perched awkwardly on the apartment's narrow spiral stairs after their first sexual encounter, Mark wonders aloud, "Why did you do this to me?" unwittingly caricaturing the self-pitying "good guy" driven to do bad deeds by a conniving woman. (True to form, this scene, while generally well composed in two shots and close-ups, includes one wide shot that slowly dollies right for no apparent reason.)

But for me the weirdest part of *The Room*—the part I really lose sleep thinking about—is that it is in fact possible that Chris-R's gun *does* come back, that there is maybe an unarticulated, unintentional setup to a later payoff working in that drug-dealer scene after all. At the end of the confrontation, Mark takes the gun from Chris-R, and as they haul him off the rooftop, Johnny says, "Let's take him to the police"; one assumes that's what happens, and hence the gun most likely gets confiscated by the cops. Yet certain things do not add up in this interpretation of the gun's fate, for if the police are brought in, why do they never show up to arrest (or at least question) Denny? Are we really to believe Chris-R doesn't spill to the cops that Denny is involved with drugs (selling them, presumably)? And he seems pretty adamant about getting that money back, given how many times he shouts, "Where's my fucking money, Denny?!" into Denny's ear. At a bare minimum, Chris-R himself ought to return later in the film to pick up where he left off with his threats. Instead, Chris-R exits the film, and we never concretely see what happens to the gun.

In the later payoff scene, when Johnny finally commits suicide, he does so with a gun that he finds in a small box that has conveniently fallen to the floor during his trashing of the condo. In true *The Room* fashion, it is not made clear why the naively trusting Johnny would even possess a gun in the first place or where exactly this one has been stashed the whole time. As Sestero puts it, Johnny "somehow gets his hands on a gun"[4] just in time for the suicide scene. But this is what makes me crazy: the gun Johnny uses to kill himself *looks exactly like the one Chris-R pulls on Denny.*

It's worth slightly digressing here to point out that both guns appear to be silver .44-caliber Auto-Mag short-recoil semiautomatic pistols, a model pervasive in crime films from the 1980s and 1990s, especially among gang members meant to be read as tough (e.g., Chris-R). Perhaps only the most astute or gun-savvy viewers would know, as I recently learned, that the limited-production gun would have been outdated by the early 2000s, the time of *The Room*'s filming; consequently, the model would have cost between $3,500 and $4,500 at the time, an astronomical sum for a handgun. The price and rarity of the model would have made it a collector's firearm, not something to keep in the home for self-defense—much less use as a film prop. All of this suggests that the gun Johnny uses to kill himself is in fact the same one brandished by Chris-R or that the presence of an identical gun in Johnny's bedroom is yet another example of the film's misuse of cliché and convention, albeit an impressively obscure one.

I am fairly certain that the film does not consciously intend me to interpret the gun Johnny offs himself with as Chris-R's gun. Yet I cannot shake the feeling that it is.

I know that the real reason for this visual rhyme between the two guns is simply that Wiseau-Films only possessed one prop gun when it made *The Room* and thus used the same prop twice. I know, on some level, that I should not make too much out of what is essentially a bad production design choice. Yet my expectations, conditioned as they are by decades spent watching Hollywood cinema, lead me to feel that within the world of the film, it is more plausible that Johnny somehow took and kept Chris-R's gun for himself off-screen than it is that he just happens to own the exact same make and model. It's like a phantom limb: I want there to be some narrative logic, some sense of setup and payoff, some assertion of that inexorable sense of cause and effect that drives most Hollywood film stories, so I imagine it into existence between the scenes of *The Room*. Chris-R's gun haunts me.

Yet this fluke result of Wiseau's slapdash methods functions as an accidental source of the movie's enduring power. By brashly calling attention to the ways in which it incompetently fails to fill narrative gaps,

The Room parodies Hollywood film narrative conventions via negative example. And by denying the logic of cause and effect, it calls attention to the contingent nature of that logic. Chris-R's gun—which both is and isn't the gun Johnny kills himself with, more Schrodinger's than Chekhov's—is another microcosmic yet paradigmatic example of *The Room* as the ultimate self-parody of a Hollywood movie.

Johnny's climactic room trashing is similarly illuminating. Though Sestero reports that James Dean was Tommy's inspiration for dramatic moments like this, I get a *Citizen Kane*–type vibe from Johnny's stiff-legged, awkward, low-energy trashing. Wiseau's homage (intentional or no) to a similar scene in *Kane* supports Bissell's point that *The Room* basically understands Hollywood conventions but that its badness arises from its inability to apply them properly, to judge tone. Despite its intended gravitas, the film's echo of *Kane* feels ridiculous, silly, satirical.

After the trashing, as he prepares to commit his final, fatal act in his bedroom, Johnny utters another one of my favorite lines in the film. "Why is this happening to me?" he moans in despair as he clutches the fateful silver gun. It is happening because Tommy Wiseau willfully made it so—he made this scene and this movie just as he intended to. We can never know what the exact nature of that intent may have been—did he mean the film to be in earnest, as seemed to be the case originally, or was Wiseau in on the joke, as he later claimed? In any case, in the on-screen world of the film, Johnny's "Why is this happening to me?" is meant to be freighted with the greatest possible existential angst, a rail directed at one's god or at fate itself—yet it is delivered by Wiseau as Johnny, a man who cannot give a convincing line reading to save his life. After we witness this performance, those somber, weighty lines from classic movie history suddenly take on a new interpretation. One can practically picture Johnny uttering, "You can't handle the truth!" or "Not the bees!"

Can it be pure coincidence that *The Room* calls out to *Vertigo* and *Citizen Kane*, two of the greatest English-language films ever made? Of course not. Through *The Room*, Tommy Wiseau shows us that he knows, in some opaque or obtuse way, the conventions of the aesthetic tradition from which his work springs. He is, in his own way, an auteur. Is he as skilled or talented as Welles or Hitchcock? Of course not. His script is outlandishly terrible, his casting skills questionable, and his film every bit the amateurish, bewilderingly bad movie that keeps fans like me coming back again and again to sup on its ironic pleasures. But that's just it: by making his own auteurist statement in the form of a clichéd Hollywood male melodrama, and by doing it so amazingly badly, Wiseau has created a lasting piece of movie parody that will endure, in its own low-cultural, cult-media fashion, as long as the works of Hitchcock, Welles, or Hollywood writ large still matter to our culture.

CARTER SOLES is Associate Professor of Film Studies in the English Department at SUNY Brockport. His work appears in *Jump Cut* and *Interdisciplinary Studies in Literature and the Environment*.

Notes

1. Bissell, "Cinema Crudité," 58–65.
2. Sestero and Bissell, *Disaster Artist*, 232.
3. Sestero and Bissell, *Disaster Artist*, 203–4.
4. Sestero and Bissell, *Disaster Artist*, 230.

2 DO YOU UNDERSTAND LIFE? DO YOU?

TOMMY WISEAU AND THE ANTI-METHOD ACTING STYLE

JAMES CURNOW

After watching *The Room* for the first time, many people find themselves in the overwhelming position of trying to articulate the cinematic event they have just witnessed. What is the secret of Tommy Wiseau's train-wreck phenomenon? How has it surpassed mere badness and become something more than the sum of its parts? Is it the screenplay? The plot holes? The strange man-child at the center of the story? Or is it the director's inability to start a scene without people entering a room and greeting each other? There are many theories, but I believe none of those things would mean anything without the narcissistic glow that emanates from the actor-director's highly distracted and emotionally erratic central performance.

We've all got our favorite Wiseau acting moments. Some favor the sight of Wiseau's bobbing butt cheeks in those torturous sex scenes. Others are drawn to the joyous laughter with which he greets a tale of domestic abuse. And for some the true glory of his performance resides more generally in the way he combines a monotonal drawl with sudden counterintuitive moments of tonal inflection ("I did NAAAAT!"). I propose that there is something more to the horrendousness of Wiseau's performance in *The Room* than meets the eye (or ear). There is a special kind of meaningful travesty at play here, one that ties back—unlikely as it may seem—to the great Hollywood method actors of the twentieth century.

The Room is, at its heart, Wiseau's attempt to replicate the emotive power generated by the likes of Marlon Brando and James Dean in their most pivotal performances. The problem is that he is completely unable to conceive of what this means at either a practical or theoretical level, instead imagining that method acting is primarily about the uncontrolled and unfocused release of the actor's own emotional energy. I propose that somehow, in the gap between his aspirations and his incompetence, Tommy Wiseau has invented an entirely new approach to acting: the anti-method.

In *The Disaster Artist: My Life inside* The Room, *the Greatest Bad Movie Ever Made,* Greg Sestero provides a vivid account of his experiences working with his friend Tommy Wiseau on *The Room*. We learn that early on in their friendship, while visiting Wiseau's apartment, Sestero came across a number of "books about acting, the Stanislavski method, Brando, and James Dean."[1] More than simply revealing a general interest in method acting and a couple of great actors, these books, Sestero would soon discover, hinted at Wiseau's obsessions. Sestero was also fascinated by Dean, and on various occasions, the men ventured out on a pilgrimage to the site of the great method actor's fatal car accident, visited one of his favorite restaurants, and discussed what it was that made James Dean special. For Wiseau, it was obvious: "He's very, you know, moment to moment. He's emotion. Real emotion. Not plastic. From the heart. Words are secondary. The way he speak. Style. And that's what you need. Don't be jealous. You can do it."[2]

Sestero also made it clear that "Tommy's dream had always been to be like Brando."[3] Perhaps that was why he sought out and signed up for the Stella Adler Academy in Los Angeles. Adler had been one of Brando's key acting coaches and also one of the three great teachers now identified with method acting in the United States. Unfortunately for Wiseau, who signed up believing that he would train under Adler, she

2.1 The famous "You are tearing me apart, Lisa!" scene. © 2003 by Wiseau-Films. (Movie still from *The Room*.)

had been dead for a decade by the time he attended classes and had had absolutely no affiliation with the academy while alive.

These two great method actors are widely acknowledged to be giants within the acting profession. Tommy Wiseau has always been acutely aware of this, and he dreamed of being seen in a similar light. As Sestero notes in *The Disaster Artist*, Wiseau was enchanted with these actors' ability "to yell" and "to floor it." But—crucially—he failed to recognize that part of their genius also came from knowing when to pull back. His key takeaway from his heroes' storied careers was that "you had to floor it for the duration of every scene."[4] For Wiseau, this is what method acting was all about.

All of this discussion raises a question: What exactly is method acting? In short, it's an acting philosophy based on the teachings of renowned early twentieth-century Russian acting teacher Konstantin Stanislavski. Stanislavski proposed a system that moved beyond the idea of acting as a mere physical craft, insisting that true authenticity required an actor to modify their own internal psychological state to align with the needs of the performance. As part of this technique, Stanislavski encouraged actors to stay in character, an approach that is still frequently adopted to this day.

Stanislavski's system was later expanded on and popularized in the United States by Adler, Lee Strasberg, and Sanford Meisner, each of whom became a giant in the theory and practice of acting. While they agreed on many of the same fundamentals and are all now generally understood to be the most influential proponents of method acting, each emphasized the value of different practices. There is not enough room here to do justice to the teachings of these three titans, but here is a brief account of the areas on which each placed the greatest importance.

For Strasberg, a theater actor turned revered acting coach of the Group Theatre during the 1930s and the director of the Actor's Studio in the 1950s, the greatest challenge for an actor was to deliver a performance without artifice.[5] The only way to do this, he suggested, was to connect the actor's own emotional memories and feelings to those of the character being portrayed. Having done so, the actor has no need for pretension; the performance becomes true. This technique, which can prove emotionally distressing for an actor, especially when practiced consistently, is what is technically known as the method, even though method acting is now broadly associated with all three of Stanislavski's most famous devotees. Among Strasberg's massive list of famous students are the likes of Al Pacino, Paul Newman, and, of course, James Dean.

Adler, an actress and former student of Strasberg, formed the Stella Adler Studio of Acting in 1949. She taught an expansion of Stanislavski's theories that focused on the importance of practical (rather than emotional) knowledge and experience in exploring a role, a process that she referred to as "defictionalizing the fiction."[6] In other words, the actor must feel so comfortable in the practical reality of their role that they can slide into it.

According to this philosophy, for somebody playing a mechanic, rudimentary practical experience working in a garage will yield a greater sense of confidence and authenticity in their performance. If they wish to play a cowboy, they should have a convincing level of comfort and aptitude in riding horses. Marlon Brando and Robert De Niro were both students of Adler and proponents of her techniques.

Finally, from Sanford Meisner came the Meisner technique. Meisner believed in "living truthfully under imaginary circumstances," by which he meant to emphasize the importance of abandoning intellectual pretension in favor of acting intuitively in the moment.[7] To that end, he developed a series of exercises that actors could use to help themselves set aside self-consciousness in their performance and live "truthfully."

Is Any Method Possible in this Madness?

It's almost impossible to imagine Wiseau applying any of these techniques. Even a peripheral glance at *The Room* reveals that he struggles with the fundamentals of acting, let alone method acting, which requires an even greater command of oneself. What is the purpose of acting? What does it mean to understand, explore, and communicate the nature of a character to an audience? Sestero provides illuminating answers to these complex questions in *The Disaster Artist*. During an acting class attended by Sestero and Wiseau, the latter was asked to perform the infamous "Stella!" scene from Tennessee Williams's play *A Streetcar Named Desire*, made famous by Brando. By Sestero's account, Wiseau proceeded to scream "Stella!" countless times, sob uncontrollably at random intervals, and abandon any commitment to the script or the integrity of the narrative. His appalled acting coach was quick to point out that while Wiseau wailed her name uncontrollably, he seemed to have totally forgotten about Stella, the intended object of his affections with whom he shared the stage. For Wiseau, it seems that acting was a kind of narcissistic pressure-release valve rather than a means of conveying any kind of meaning to an audience.

Of course, in *The Room* this narcissism plays out in ways that push far beyond the boundaries of mere acting. The film takes place in a universe in which all other characters live in the orbit of Johnny (played by Wiseau). There are just two poles in this universe: At one end are those characters who live in a state of adoration of Johnny, from the shop assistant who kicks off the movie by declaring Johnny her "favorite customer," to the adoring Denny, who sees Johnny as a "father figure," and to the character of Mark, who is declared to be Johnny's "best friend" on no less than seven occasions. At the other end lie "evil" people like Lisa, Johnny's fiancée. Mark's affair with her is the catalyst for Johnny's descent into self-pity and despair, prompting his rather broad and unwarranted declaration that "Everybody betray me!" But Lisa, whom Wiseau has unevenly written as oscillating among emotionally confused, sociopathic, and stalkerish, certainly *has* betrayed him. To make this crystal clear, Wiseau has her declare that she doesn't love Johnny five times and that she loves Mark ten.

How could it be, we are asked, that any woman could possibly betray this superb best friend, father figure, and model customer? It's clear that for Wiseau the problem in no way lives within the character of Johnny but within the people who do not appreciate him as others do. Given this rigid, binary perspective, it's hard to imagine how Wiseau could ever interrogate the complex nature of a character and deliver a performance with any kind of verisimilitude.

Ironically, James Franco's use of method acting in his portrayal of Tommy Wiseau in Franco's film adaptation of *The Disaster Artist* helps him convey this very obtuseness. The technique enabled him to delve beneath the awkward and often comical facade of his subject to portray a convincing interpretation of the notoriously impenetrable human being underneath. Franco's Wiseau is an almost infantile creature, prone to extreme selfishness and self-involvement, overly possessive emotional attachment, spontaneous outbursts, and an almost unfeasibly reductive view of the world. But this is also a man of unusual curiosity, ingenuity, and aspiration, fundamentally limited by some kind of stunted emotional intelligence. Wiseau is captivated by the human condition but completely unable to access or interpret its mechanics. I'd argue that in Franco's and Sestero's interpretations of Wiseau's character, we're given a vital key to understanding what makes Tommy Wiseau's acting technique truly special. And that key is the anti-method.

Let me begin by stating that the anti-method requires a performer's earnest and heartfelt attempt to emotionally express the human condition through acting. It must begin from a sincere, honest place, a place Wiseau certainly reaches in *The Room*. The actor must aspire to create an emotional connection among the actor, the character, and the audience. There is no doubt that this aspiration lies at the very heart of Wiseau's performance. But most importantly, like Wiseau, the anti-method actor must, by any reasonable measure, fail to achieve this aspiration in spectacular fashion.

Existing in absolute contradiction with the teachings of Strasberg, Adler, and Meisner, the anti-method technique is to be achieved in three fundamental steps.

Step One: Create an Emotional Disconnection

Strasberg advised actors to search their memories and emotions for experiences that might align at some level with those of the character they seek to play. For the anti-method practitioner, it is important to have an almost complete lack of insight into the internal mechanics of their own mind, and more generally those of the human condition, so they have no reference point for their character. They must seek to make those connections but be left entirely wanting. Instead, the actor must use every moment as a point of narcissistic primal self-expression through which to expel emotions they are unable to articulate in any intelligible or socially redeeming way.

On some level, disconnecting from the human condition should be something of a challenge for Wiseau in the context of *The Room*. If we are to understand his screenplay as an attempt to articulate some deep feeling of undeserved betrayal, autobiographical or not, then at the very least we might expect that Wiseau should not have too much trouble in summoning up emotions and experiences to feed into his role. From being looked over for a promotion to learning about the affair between his fiancée and best friend, the character of Johnny is articulating the heart of the play when he screams, "Everybody betray me! I fed up with this world!" (This topic is explored at length in chapter 5.)

Despite all this, when it comes time to perform, Wiseau appears to be entirely unable to express any feeling or modulate his behavior accordingly in any useful way. He cannot read the tone of a scene, his character, or even his own body. Instead, Wiseau rotates through three key types of emotive misfire:

- The delivery of emotionally expressive dialogue in a monotonal form. The best example of this is the infamous scene in which Johnny bursts into a rooftop shot blandly moaning, "I did not hit her! It's not true! It's bullshit! I did not hit her! I did not!" before looking off-screen, changing inexplicably to an upbeat tone and declaring, "Oh, hi Mark."
- The expression of inappropriate emotions. A perfect example occurs when Mark recounts a story to Johnny regarding a promiscuous woman beaten to the point of hospitalization. When Mark is finished, Johnny bursts out laughing and joyously exclaims, "What a story, Mark!"
- The overaccentuation of emotions in awkward ways. Take the scene in which the troubled Denny, having nearly been killed by a drug dealer, is being consoled by Lisa and Johnny. Johnny holds young Denny close, pressing his cheek against the top of the boy's head (see fig. 2.2). As Lisa tells him, "Denny, you know that Johnny's like your father," Wiseau attempts a pained and paternal closed-eyed expression that gives the distinct impression he may be having a large orgasm.

Step Two: Embrace a State of Intellectual Ignorance

While Adler recommended that the actor seek out knowledge and experiences that will better inform the practical realities of a role, the anti-method actor must instead attempt to maximize their ignorance of every element of their character's personal reality. This will provide

2.2 Johnny takes Denny under his wing. © 2003 by Wiseau-Films. (Movie still from *The Room*.)

a sense of alienated distance that will highlight the actor's complete unfamiliarity with the role.

In the case of Wiseau, this step *should* be the most difficult. He could not be ignorant of the script because he wrote it, and so the preparations required to master the role should be front of mind. If Johnny likes football, then Wiseau should be comfortable throwing a football. If Johnny is a banker, then Wiseau should be able to convey this convincingly. And frankly, if Wiseau has ever had a friend, he should be capable of some kind of vaguely convincing interaction with his "best friend." Yet somehow Wiseau's performance demonstrates his complete disengagement from the practical realities of acting out his own script.

Johnny clearly loves football, as evidenced by his interest in playing catch in several scenes throughout the movie. And yet each throw he makes looks like the clumsy act of somebody who's encountered the sport for the first time just hours earlier. Similarly, when Johnny interacts with his "best friend," Mark, he is incapable of communicating any sense of camaraderie, instead leaning on the repetition of this phrase to ensure the audience's acknowledgment of their relationship. And when Johnny complains about the first of the betrayals he suffers in the film—being overlooked for a promotion at his bank—he delivers his lines in the staccato fashion of a computer-generated voice reading a script, providing this rather unconvincing account of what happened: "That son of a bitch told me that I would get it within three months. I save them bundles. They're crazy. I don't think I will ever get it. They betray me, they didn't keep their promise, they tricked me, and I don't care anymore."

Never in acting history has any actor seemed less attached to the words coming out of their own mouth than at this moment. If viewers watched just this one scene, they might assume that Wiseau spoke no English and learned his lines phonetically.

Step Three: Become One with Absolute Pretension

The anti-method actor must genuinely aspire to live in the moment of the performance, just as Sanford Meisner encouraged. To help achieve this, Meisner insightfully encouraged actors to clear their minds to allow for an authentic performance delivered raw and true in the moment. The anti-method actor, though, must work to achieve this effect through a poor facsimile of the physicality and mannerisms of a well-recognized method actor at their peak. This has the added *intended* but deeply ironic benefit of conveying authenticity by borrowing it from somebody else.

In the case of Wiseau, the actor seems most eager to borrow his authenticity from James Dean. The most literal clue to this lies in the direct homage to Dean's performance in *Rebel Without a Cause* within *The Room*. At one point, as confused as the audience is by Lisa's sudden rejection of Johnny, he screams, "You're tearing me apart, Lisa!" as he brings his forearms in to shield his face in an expression of gathering madness. Dean recites almost the same line in *Rebel Without a Cause*, and he does so with a similar kind of jagged hyperexpressiveness. But in Wiseau's inept and derivative hands, the moment appears inappropriate, awkward, and severe. Just as when he attempted to emulate Brando in *A Streetcar Named Desire* years earlier, he is incapable of understanding his source material beyond its being a brilliant moment of primal expression.

That said, this moment does have a function, albeit not one Wiseau intended—it serves as a clue to the secret of his performance throughout the film: When Johnny bursts clumsily into a scene protesting his innocence regarding Lisa's domestic violence allegations. When he attacks Mark at his party. When he destroys his living room. And when he thrusts his pelvis into the red dress of his treacherous fiancée while weeping and screaming "Why?" repeatedly at the universe before blowing his brains out.

In each and every one of these scenes, Wiseau pulls on the emotive peaks of Dean's performance in *Rebel Without a Cause*. He takes the adolescent angst that Dean was giving expression to for the first time and the hyperexpressive elements that would have been perceived as realist in the context of the 1950s. He takes Dean's sharp and exaggerated movements. He takes his sudden explosive teenage outbursts. And then Wiseau flattens it all, ironing out its life, meaning, and technique, and wears it like a shroud.

This last point is critical. Without this ill-fitting shroud, Wiseau would merely have delivered an unrecognizable mess of excessive and inappropriate emotional venting. But with it, his performance becomes a disturbing, comical, and parodic approximation of method acting. It is this visage that signals to the viewer both what was intended and how far from that intention the final result has landed.

By replicating this approach, an actor may deliver a meaningless and unfocused performance that's paradoxically both emotive and banal, terrible and fascinating. This collision of forces, when perfected, achieves the status of the anti-method. In prioritizing navel-gazing and untempered emotive expression while subtly referencing the very elements that can make a performance great, the anti-method is first and foremost a technique that invariably and unintentionally satirizes the worst of acting.

Conclusion

It's interesting to ponder whether there are other actors who might retrospectively be considered practitioners of the anti-method. Ed Wood may have come close with *Glen or Glenda* (1953), his cinematic exploration of his own predilection toward cross-dressing. But in that film Wood proves himself to be surprisingly introspective despite his awful artistic instincts. Does Steven Seagal's straight-faced sincerity attain the necessary train-wreck irony in *On Deadly Ground* (1994) to become a member of this elite club? Did Brando transition from method to anti-method with *The Island of Dr. Moreau* (1996), in which he delivered a lazy and narcissistic performance that appeared to parody his own work in *Apocalypse Now* (1979)? It's possible. But at no point in cinematic history has an actor so convincingly embodied the collision of ambition and incompetence as did Tommy Wiseau in *The Room*.

That is the secret of Wiseau's achievement. It is his instinctive understanding that acting is a form of emotional expression, combined with his inability to conceive of the purpose of this expression or ways to wield it. It is Wiseau's correct intuition that within the performances of the great method actors there is something special that relates to personal expression, although he cannot decipher what that special thing is. And most importantly, it's the fact that Tommy Wiseau, with all of his limitations, chose to attempt to deliver something rich and meaningful. Through the process of the anti-method, he achieved something both beautiful and grotesque, its contradictions ultimately bringing him success beyond his wildest dreams, albeit in a different way than he imagined.

JAMES CURNOW is Editor of CURNBLOG.com. He holds a PhD in Film and Television from Monash University.

Notes

1. Sestero and Bissell, *Disaster Artist*, 55.
2. Sestero and Bissell, *Disaster Artist*, 76.
3. Sestero and Bissell, *Disaster Artist*, 265.
4. Sestero and Bissell, *Disaster Artist*, 58.
5. Brestoff, *Great Acting Teachers and Their Methods*.
6. Adler, *Technique of Acting*, 26.
7. Meisner and Longwell, *Sanford Meisner on Acting*, 15.

3 "SHE CAN'T LOVE ANYONE"

THE EVIL WOMEN AND TORMENTED MEN OF THE ROOM

LENIKA CRUZ

There is something perverse yet fitting about the fact that a movie as claustrophobic and insular as *The Room* opens with several shots of sweeping outdoor vistas. The waters of the San Francisco Bay twinkle. A languid haze hugs the skyline. Trolleys crawl across the city as a lilting piano score dances in the background. A glimpse of the Golden Gate Bridge, known for its high rates of suicide, foreshadows the morbid escape that the film's lead character, Johnny—a man forsaken by everyone around him—will seek at the end of the story.

The expansiveness of these exterior shots only amplifies the suffocating, stale energy of the movie's interior scenes, which make up the vast majority of the film. Watching it, no one would be surprised that the writer, director, and star, Tommy Wiseau, initially conceived of his "disasterpiece" as a stage play set in a single location. Containment seems to be the governing principle of *The Room*. Characters work to bury their feelings and beliefs deep inside while trying to cover up their misdeeds. Their motivations are often inscrutable. Everyone has secrets. It's all too fitting that so many of these characters express deeply simplistic worldviews, the kind that seem utterly unexposed to the oxidizing, complicating air of, well, reality.

In particular, *The Room* presents a cynical and reductive vision of how men and women relate to one another—that is, exclusively through the lens of romantic relationships. The film begins by embracing the rigidity of conventional, heteronormative gender roles and doubles (and triples) down on them through the entire length of the movie. In its telling, men are providers whose ability to offer financial support and emotional affirmation to women all but entitles men to marriage and a comfortable life. Women, meanwhile, are largely confined to the domestic sphere, tasked with maintaining the home and sexually satisfying men.

This is a film with no apparent skepticism of the gender binary. *The Room* articulates what makes a man *a man*, and what makes a woman *a woman*, by having characters of the same gender talk about the other gender in closed settings. Women literally talk in rooms together about men, and men literally talk in rooms together about women. The result is a dynamic in which the interactions between men and women throughout the movie are reduced to bizarre performances of stereotypical gender roles.

The movie's values are announced from the very first scene. When the movie begins, Johnny (Wiseau) arrives home after work and presents his fiancée, Lisa (Juliette Danielle), a red dress as a gift. Perhaps triggered on some visceral level by the dress, as women are, Lisa immediately wants to make love, which leads to the first of several painfully protracted sex scenes. The scene is like an erotica novel brought to life. We glimpse the couple through obscuring elements such as waterfalls and white veils and curtains, but the romance of the scene is *really* emphasized by all the usual symbols of romantic love: red roses, dripping red candles, R & B music. ("I would stand in the way of a bullet . . . just to show you I love you, I will," goes the first song, as Johnny and Lisa make love in the room where Johnny will indeed later put himself in front of a bullet as his final expression of how his love for Lisa has destroyed him.)[1] The scene is meant to convey just what a happy couple Johnny and Lisa are: *Look at how thoughtful he is to buy her a gift just because he believes she's so beautiful. Look what an amazing man he is. Look how sexually open Lisa is, how passionately and theatrically they have sex on an average weeknight.* When Johnny wakes up the next morning and strides to the bathroom totally naked, Lisa wakes up, sees a rose lying on his pillow, smiles to no one, and pulls it to her nose for a sniff. *Who does that?* A blissfully happy woman. Right?

Wrong. After Johnny leaves for work, the first of the film's single-gender scenes takes place, with the goal of establishing Lisa's sociopathy. When Lisa's mother, Claudette (Carolyn Minnott), stops by, Lisa's demeanor has suddenly transformed. "I don't love him anymore," she tells Claudette, confessing her unhappiness with Johnny but admitting, "I don't mind living with him." Claudette is horrified, reminding Lisa of what a good provider he is ("He bought you a car, a ring, clothes, whatever you wanted") and urging her not to break up with him. After some childish whining, Lisa allows that her mother may be right. "Of course I'm right," Claudette responds. "I *know* men. I wasn't born yesterday."

Throughout the film, Claudette will continue to present herself as an authority on men; she comes across as a woman who has suffered mightily because of men but who views that suffering as the natural state of things. In a later scene, she tells Lisa she hasn't been happy since meeting her first husband, adding that she didn't even want to marry Lisa's father. Lisa is upset by this revelation, but Claudette says coldly, "Men and women use and abuse each other; there's nothing wrong with it. Marriage has nothing to do with love" (see fig. 3.1). Lisa, meanwhile, is idealistic and believes she deserves real love, happiness, and excitement—which in itself isn't so bad, except that the movie goes out of its way to depict her as selfish, confused, deceptive, and volatile for wanting this. Of course, Johnny—and Wiseau himself, if we treat the character as his proxy[2]—*also* has an idealistic approach to love, albeit one that's different from Lisa's and somehow even more simplistic. "If a lot of people loved each other, the world would be a better place to

3.1 Claudette and Lisa have a talk. © 2003 by Wiseau-Films. (Movie still from *The Room*.)

live," according to his famous line. As for Claudette, *The Room* tries to portray her perspective on men and women as toxic, but ironically the story winds up validating her worldview completely. In fact, we might even think of her as channeling the movie's (Wiseau's) *real* views on relationships.

There's plenty of evidence in the film to support Claudette's beliefs. From the beginning, the dynamic between men and women is transactional. The first interaction between Lisa and Johnny's best friend,

Mark (Greg Sestero), involves Lisa calling Mark out of the blue to get something out of him. Despite his protests of being very busy, Lisa insists that they talk right away, in person: "You owe me one anyway," she says, though it's not clear why he would owe her anything. He visits her, appearing willfully naive and oblivious as she circles him, like prey. Eventually, he catches on: "The candles, the music, the sexy dress. What's going on here?" he asks.

Mark gives in to her advances, and they have sex on the stairs as R & B music like the kind that came on during Johnny and Lisa's first lovemaking scene plays in the background. Afterward, Mark sighs. "Why did you do this to me? Johnny is my best friend," he says, establishing Lisa as the primary actor with agency and Mark as a helpless victim. She is a succubus and the catalyst for all the horrors to come. She exists to take things from people.

Later, when Johnny comes home with red roses for Lisa (again with the gifts!), upset about not having gotten a promotion at work, Lisa throws an impromptu drunken pizza party and implores him to make love to her. He grunts with disinterest, prompting her to say, "Come on. You owe me one." Lisa's strange entitlement to sex inverts the typical understanding of men as the ones who do the desiring and thus casts her as deviant and pathological.

In a world where women are as mysterious as Lisa and Claudette, the men of *The Room* often turn to one another for affirmation and advice about navigating the other sex. In the famous rooftop scene one-third of the way through the film, Mark furtively asks Johnny, "Do you think girls like to cheat like guys do?" It's an interesting question, one that acknowledges the double standard at work—even though the men in the film never openly discuss their own supposedly innate impulse to cheat. To illustrate his theory about women liking to cheat, Mark tells a story: "I knew this girl; she had a dozen guys. One of them found out about it and beat her up so bad, she ended up in a hospital on Guerrero Street." If the tale was primarily intended to illustrate how disgustingly promiscuous some women are, it also foreshadows the violence that men can turn to when they're cuckolded—the violence that Johnny himself will turn to at the end but direct at himself. There's a sobering lesson to be learned here, but none of the men will receive it. They can't because they exist as hyperexaggerated "men," or what Wiseau believes "men" to be.

If Mark and Johnny's rooftop conversation lays the foundation for *The Room*'s theory of womanhood (and manhood), later discussions between Johnny and his (male) friends add the bricks. When talking with his psychologist friend, Peter, Johnny confesses, "I don't understand women. Do you, Peter?" "What man does?" Peter replies conspiratorially. "They never say what they mean, and they always play games." Once again, women are liars and utter enigmas to men. Then, of course, Mark walks in. "We're just talking about women," Johnny says, at which the mood darkens instantly. "Women just confuse me," Mark confides, going on to obliquely reference his troubles with Lisa, making sure he mentions that she's both unfaithful and beautiful: "She's married, she's very attractive. It's driving me crazy." Not long after, Mark and Peter have a private conversation on the roof, during which Mark smokes marijuana and abruptly attacks Peter because of his anguish over Lisa. He apologizes, but still finds a way to blame Lisa. "She's such a manipulative bitch; this is all her fault," Mark screams. "Fuck!" The implication is clear: Mark, unlike Lisa, feels incredible guilt about their relationship, meaning that he at least has a conscience, a moral compass.

Men plus women seems to equal disaster in *The Room*. Only one couple in the film is shown as happy: Johnny's friend Mike and Lisa's friend Michelle. How do we know they're happy? Though they only appear in a few scenes together, we see that their relationship is uninhibited, honest, and very sexual (of course). They're frequently shown feeding each other food in a teasingly romantic way, as a kind of foreplay.

Michelle's main function in the film is to serve as an important foil to Lisa—she is a seemingly "good" woman who is faithful and happy in her relationship with Mike. But even Michelle is at first somewhat permissive of Lisa's cruel attitude toward Johnny, even if she's bewildered by it. "You have to take as much as you can. I just want to live, live, live," Lisa tells her, as if spelling out her manifesto. *The Room,* clearly, is disturbed by the notion of a woman who conflates "living" with total selfishness, a woman who is willing to reject the comfort, safety, and dignity of marriage in pursuit of some misguided vision of liberation. "Don't worry, your secret is safe with me," Michelle responds—just as Johnny walks in. His unexpected appearance threatens to permeate the wall that has thus far concealed women's true motivations and mindsets from men. "I heard you, Michelle, what secret?" Johnny asks. "It's between us women. It's girl talk," Lisa snaps. *It's girl talk*—the kind of sentence no woman would speak in earnest. Indeed, the preceding scene between Lisa and Michelle plays out like what a man might imagine women talk about when they're alone.

In the fight between Johnny and Lisa that erupts after Michelle leaves, *The Room* underscores what it finds so terrifying about women. "You shouldn't have any secrets from me," Johnny implores Lisa, reminding her that they're about to get married. She's unfazed. "Women change their minds all the time," Lisa responds menacingly. The fact that they've been together for seven years hangs heavy over the scene—as does Lisa's recklessness and disinterest in their history together. As much as *The Room* drags on, there's never a scene that hints at what precipitating event could explain Lisa's sudden interest in Mark or her disgust with Johnny. "Women change their minds all the time" is as close to an explanation as *The Room* gives for her change of heart. Lisa's behavior feels genuinely inexplicable, evidence that women are as unknowable as Peter, Johnny, and Mark believe them to be.

This belief is at the root of Johnny's (and the movie's) paranoia about heterosexual romantic relationships, the idea that women can turn on men at any time, for no good reason. "Man, I just can't figure women out," Mark laments in one of the rooftop scenes. "Sometimes they're just too smart, sometimes they're just flat-out stupid, other times they're just evil."

It's worth noting just how much the conversations between men and the conversations between women diverge from one another. Not all of the men's interactions have to do with women—they spend plenty of time bonding, jogging together, tossing a football around. Not so the women. *The Room* easily and hilariously fails the Bechdel-Wallace test,[3] one of the more popular (if necessarily limited) ways of assessing depictions of female characters in fiction. Only the conversations between women turn extremely conniving or ugly, and they exclusively center on men. ("I have him wrapped around my little finger," Lisa tells Michelle with a giggle, as if that's a perfectly normal and OK thing to admit.) The film depends on all the characters remaining in their silos. The womanly secrets between Lisa, Claudette, and Michelle need to exist in their own world, just as the beliefs that Mark, Peter, Johnny, and Denny hold about women must never be challenged and only affirmed.

It makes sense that everything finally explodes at the birthday party near the end. It's the most mixed-gender scene in the film, with men and women all mingling together. With everyone under the same roof, the boundaries have been weakened, and the different story lines are bleeding together. The partygoers are doing their best to keep up appearances, to perform their roles as "happy fiancée," "happy birthday boy," "happy best friend." "Lisa looks hot tonight," one random man comments, unprompted, to the woman next to him: *Look!* the film seems to say. *Lisa's evil allure knows no bounds.* At last, all the characters are stuck in the pressure cooker of Johnny and Lisa's house. (Only Mike and Michelle, the perfect couple, seem perfectly at ease with each other.) Even Lisa's repeated attempts to get everyone to go outside can't equalize the pressure.

Finally, the boundaries are irreversibly breached: Steven, an entirely new character intended to replace Peter, catches Lisa and Mark making out inside the house. Johnny announces to the guests a poisonous piece of fiction that Lisa fed to him: the couple is expecting a baby. It's the trigger that sets the film's final, calamitous act into motion. Even as Lisa has been pulling away from her boring life with Johnny, she has also been conjuring up the last piece needed to complete the picture of a typical, heteronormative nuclear family: a child. It's a lie that will prove untenable. "I only told him that to make it interesting," Lisa tells Steven and Michelle when they confront her about her recklessness. "I feel like I'm sitting on an atomic bomb waiting for it to go off," Steven responds darkly, but Lisa doesn't heed his warning.

In the next scene, Mark and Lisa are suddenly brave and unrepentant in their desire for each other, forcing Johnny to intercede. "If you kept your girl satisfied, she wouldn't come to me!" Mark yells at Johnny, attacking him where he had believed he was secure—in the sexual satisfaction he offered to Lisa. This is the final straw; with this latest transgression, Johnny's destruction as a "man" is complete. "Everybody betray me! I fed up with this world," Johnny yells as the party comes to a halt.

The Room ends where it began: with Lisa's red dress. It symbolizes everything—the succubus, the fiery passion of love, the betrayal. Given the film's fixation on romance as the primary means by which men and women connect with one another, it only makes sense that the conclusion has strong sexual overtones. As Johnny rampages through his house, destroying everything, the film cuts back to scenes of Lisa smiling, laughing. He's tormented by these flashes of her, of his memories of the mask she presented him. The images are intrusive, whereas the film once took care to keep its characters and their anxieties over the other sex compartmentalized. The violence that *The Room* had hinted at throughout finally arrives; the atomic bomb goes off, but Johnny's violence is turned inward at himself. He, the film declares, is a pure soul who is *unlike other men*, unlike the ones who beat up their girlfriends or try to throw their friends off roofs. In one of the most disturbing scenes in the film, Johnny grabs the red dress that he gave Lisa and angrily thrusts his hips at it. Here, love and suffering are inextricable.

Once Johnny grabs the gun and pulls the trigger, the tableau is complete: red everywhere. A man undone by the deviousness of the woman he so selflessly loved. Though Johnny is framed as a kind of martyr, the casualty of Mark's and Lisa's heartlessness, his death is of course meant to hurt them. When they discover his body, Mark yells at Lisa, "Tramp, you killed him. You're the cause of all of this. I don't love you. Get out of our life, you bitch." *The Room*'s hatred for Lisa couldn't be more obvious. At last, Denny—Lisa and Johnny's surrogate child—arrives to see the gory remnants of all the lies and secrets. As the three sob, it's clear at whose feet the blame should be laid. Lisa cries, but her tears aren't meant as a reminder of her humanity. They're a reassurance to the audience that she has been punished and that Johnny has received some measure of justice in death. This woman has been put in her place.

LENIKA CRUZ is Senior Editor at the *Atlantic,* where she covers culture.

Notes

1. On a side note, if Tommy Wiseau did choose this song with the purpose of foreshadowing the ending, then he deserves at least some credit for a correctly applied storytelling technique.

2. So much commentary about *The Room,* and indeed the popularity of *The Disaster Artist* book and film, rests on conflating the character of Johnny and his creator, Tommy Wiseau. "This is real life," Sestero reports Wiseau telling him during one of their grueling filming days, according to *The Disaster Artist* book (p. 251).

3. The Bechdel-Wallace test, often shortened to just the Bechdel test, was introduced by author and illustrator Alison Bechdel in her 1985 comic book *Dykes to Watch Out For.* In the comic, a character outlines her requirements for seeing a movie: "One, it has to have at least two women in it . . . who, two, talk to each other about, three, something besides a man." What began as a wry poke at Hollywood's portrayal of women has come to be something of a widely cited yardstick for measuring female representation.

PART II
UNLOCKING *THE ROOM*

IS *THE ROOM* WORSE THAN *VERTIGO*? 4

THE AESTHETIC PHILOSOPHY OF "SO BAD IT'S GOOD"

JAMES MACDOWELL

Alfred Hitchcock's *Vertigo* and Tommy Wiseau's *The Room* could both be described the same way: as a San Francisco–set male melodrama about a man named Johnny[1] and his failure to understand the inscrutable (blonde) woman with whom he is obsessively in love. After subjecting her to numerous inquisitions, and even a program of covert surveillance, Johnny discovers that the object of his affection has been deceiving him in various ways throughout the narrative—a fact the audience has long been aware of. This discovery sends the distraught Johnny into a jealous rage, with ultimately tragic consequences. These movies have numerous other things in common, including scenes of our male protagonist aimlessly wandering San Franciscan streets, several specific locations, a narratively significant spiral staircase, and memorable moments set in flower shops.

In 2012, *Vertigo* ended *Citizen Kane*'s fifty-year reign atop *Sight & Sound* magazine's "Greatest Films of All Time" poll. By the same year, *The Room* had firmly cemented its reputation as "the *Citizen Kane* of bad movies." If I were asked to list my favorite films, both *Vertigo* and *The Room* might be among the first titles I named. Why? For the simple reason that watching them gives me great pleasure; indeed, in this respect perhaps I even love them equally. At the same time, if the subject changed from *personal pleasure* to *artistic value,* I would have to agree with their irreconcilable critical reputations: I consider *Vertigo* to be among the best films I have seen, whereas I consider *The Room* to be among the worst. But if I genuinely love them more or less equally, why am I sure that *The Room* is worse than *Vertigo*? I think that confronting this question may allow us to better understand "so bad it's good" as an aesthetic concept.

So—why do I love *The Room*? Too many reasons to count. However, chief among them is quite how hilarious, strange, and destabilizing I find its failure to achieve its ostensible central aim: to be a towering tribute from Wiseau to himself.

The Room's central project appears fundamentally to be to move its audience to sympathize with Johnny by representing him as an unfailingly good, sensitive, and loving man who becomes the undeserving victim of all around him ("How could you *do* this to me?"; "I treat you like a princess and you stab me in the back!"; "Everybody betray me!"). It fails to reach this goal, however, largely because of how ineptly the film represents every aspect of its fictional world—in particular, how unconvincingly it depicts both Johnny's virtues and other characters' betrayals. Johnny's goodness is by turns awkwardly expressed (he is established as his local florist's favorite customer, and he offers unprompted bromides like "If a lot of people loved each other, the world would be a better place"); cringe-inducingly conventional (he buys Lisa red dresses and red roses); and rather weird (he apparently has quasi-adopted a teenage boy, and he lets friends use his apartment for sex). Likewise, Wiseau's inability to dramatize recognizable social and psychological phenomena ensures that Lisa's duplicitousness is rendered in ways that appear—among other characterizations—unmotivated (the best explanation Lisa can come up with is she finds Johnny "boring"); inconsistent (her lies concerning Johnny's domestic abuse and her pregnancy are summarily dropped); and frankly unnecessary (the

4.1 Judy Barton (Kim Novak) and John "Scottie" Ferguson (James Stewart) in *Vertigo*. © 1958 by Paramount Pictures. (Movie still from *Vertigo*.)

reason proffered for why Lisa doesn't simply *leave* Johnny is that she "can't support [her]self").

So, *The Room*'s conscious project is to present Johnny/Wiseau as being undeservedly and inexplicably victimized by the devilish seductress he has the misfortune to love. In short, at the heart of the film lies a deep reservoir of self-pitying, masculinist narcissism. What I love about it, however, is that, by failing *so* spectacularly to depict this state of affairs in anything like a coherent manner, it comes to feel almost like a parody of its ideological project. The ultimate effect is to expose the movie's troubling central psychosocial conceit *as* troubling and offer it up to our ridicule. There's a reason it has become an established ritual at fan screenings to yell "Because *you're a woman*!" at the numerous moments

Lisa is reminded of her supposedly total dependence on Johnny or makes one of her many bizarrely vindictive pronouncements.

Imagine for a moment that this was all intentional. Say the film was crafted so as to create a sense that it is being told by an unreliable narrator: a storyteller who is constitutionally incapable of comprehending the people and actions depicted, especially the story's women. We are thus meant to understand that *The Room* is presenting a confusingly self-deceiving account of a run-of-the-mill breakup—a breakup for which Johnny/Wiseau in truth probably shoulders his share of blame. Imagine that this film didn't just sometimes feel oddly like, but actually *was,* a thoroughgoing parody of sexist narcissism. And imagine that all the other "mistakes" people love to mock were in fact painstakingly crafted in service of this aim. If the film supported that interpretation, it's possible I might regard *The Room* as some kind of masterpiece: no longer "so bad it's good" but actually verging on "so good it's genius."

Why isn't the film usually interpreted and evaluated in this way? Perhaps it's because we have no evidence, textual or contextual, that Wiseau did make the film with these intentions. Yet why does this matter? Aren't we long past the point in critical history when an artwork's value is assumed to reside wholly in whatever an artist consciously intended? Take *Vertigo*. Much of my love and admiration for this film stems from my awed appreciation for the extraordinary artistry evident in its construction, which produces such densely patterned interrelated meanings, elicits such stirring and complex emotional effects, and so on. At the same time, it remains true that I cannot know, for instance, to what extent *Vertigo*'s own depiction of doomed male sexual obsession is the product of Hitchcock *consciously* scrutinizing his reportedly troubling psychological issues with (and treatment of) women. And, while Hitchcock's Johnny is unquestionably regarded by his film as a far more morally ambiguous figure than Wiseau's, I cannot be sure quite how *intentionally* searing *Vertigo*'s critique of romantic love and masculine possessiveness is—despite the fact that I (and many other critics) believe this aspect of the film contributes significantly to its value.[2] I consider the film a great work of cinematic art even if these questions remain unanswerable and deem Hitchcock a great artist for having made it.

The fact that I can't, if I'm fully honest with myself, extend this same logic to *The Room* gets to the heart of what "so bad it's good" means as an aesthetic concept. Despite the faintly transgressive aura surrounding the term, enjoying something for its failings requires assenting—whether we like it or not—to some rather traditional ideas about art, including those regarding intention. It could seem that legions of fans laughing uproariously at a putative melodrama like *The Room* confirms that a text's meanings aren't determined by its author's intentions. In the philosophy of art, this position is known as anti-intentionalism. However, responding to *The Room* like this also presupposes that we can accurately surmise the movie's *original* intentions and that doing so is an important stage of the interpretive process. If we can't assume a film intended to achieve certain aims, then we can't deem it "bad" for failing in those aims and can't then recast this badness as "so bad it's good." Essentially, to enjoy it in the way I do, I *must* first assume that *The Room* wasn't intended to be a self-parodic comedy.

The same goes for the issue of artistic evaluation. Loving a film's failures might appear to support the philosophical position called subjectivism—the notion that there are no rational standards governing evaluation and that *artistic value* is simply another name for the degree of aesthetic pleasure an artwork affords us personally. But is this quite right? Appreciating *The Room* in anything like the way that I (and seemingly most others) do requires me, firstly, to believe that it aims to be an effective male melodrama rather than a parody and, secondly, to believe that its complete failure to achieve this aim makes it bad. This effectively forces me to concede that there exists at least one—if not *objective,* then at least rationally justifiable—standard for aesthetic evaluation. If calling something "so bad it's good" involves appreciating an artwork for failing to achieve its aesthetic intentions, then this fundamentally assumes that artistic *goodness* would require achieving them.

In order to call *The Room* a truly great work of cinematic art, and Wiseau a truly great artist for having made it, I would need to disregard the link between aesthetic value and intention to a vastly larger extent than for *Vertigo.* I assume that only *some* of the things I value most in *Vertigo* could wholly exceed Hitchcock and his collaborators' artistic aims; by contrast, I assume that virtually *none* of what I love about *The Room* came about intentionally. That its badness affords me fun and bemused fascination doesn't alter my negative evaluation of it—indeed, it *depends* on it. This hardly confirms subjectivist accounts of artistic value—quite the opposite: it demonstrates especially convincingly why it might make sense to treat artistic value and aesthetic pleasure as two separate things. In this sense, "so bad it's good" is actually a misnomer: it involves reevaluating not the film itself but the *experience* the film affords. A more accurate term might be "so bad it's pleasurable."[3]

What, finally, is the status of artists themselves within this philosophy of art? There might seem to be something fundamentally distasteful about treating a film as "so bad it's good." It seems to require condescending to the work and, moreover, adopting a haughtily superior attitude toward the artists behind the work. It involves assuming we're able to see failings and limitations of which artists were unaware or, for whatever reason, unable to transcend. I do think, though, that there's also something about this kind of appreciation that can't be wholly explained by this image of utterly detached, ironic condescension.

Like most fans of *The Room*, I consider it important to assume that Wiseau is responsible for the vast majority of the endless complexity, interest, and gratification I gain from the film. And in that sense, I am genuinely and deeply grateful to him for having made it. It remains true that I must view Wiseau as having produced a damning auto-critique via his Johnny only *accidentally*. However, this is also what allows the film to create for me anything like the level of pathos it's actually straining for.

The Room does, in a weird way, make me feel a kind of sympathy—not for Johnny the character but for Wiseau the flailing artist trying desperately to express himself, believing himself to be hitting it out of the park. Many of his fans can surely relate, in some fashion, to that quixotic predicament (certainly this seems to be, for instance, James Franco and Seth Rogen's motivation for making *The Disaster Artist*). For me, Wiseau's unawareness also makes *The Room* feel like a uniquely intriguing demonstration of how unquestioned ideologies can manifest in art. Of course, there's the work's barely disguised misogyny, which causes lines like "Sometimes [women] are just too smart, sometimes they're just flat-out stupid, other times they're just evil" (this, incidentally, is one reason I feel less guilty for mocking Wiseau than I otherwise might). But I also always come back to that one moment on the roof when Johnny responds to Denny's expressed desire to "graduate from college, get a good job, get married, and have kids": "That's the *idea*!" Johnny exclaims, with a patronizing yet affectionate grin. Wiseau treats this as if he were congratulating Denny on having just grasped the most self-evident truth about what human beings were put on Earth to do. It's one of the many moments when I feel Wiseau telling both us and himself, unconsciously but unmistakably, "This is the way the world is and must be, for me and for everyone, from now until the end of time." As Johnny puts it elsewhere, "That's *life*!"

Basically, then, I presume that *The Room* hints strongly at who Tommy Wiseau, the flesh-and-blood man, is. I find it interesting that, by contrast, whether Hitchcock the flesh-and-blood man saw himself in *Vertigo*'s Johnny matters far less to me. Whether he did or not, he created a film that could never be mistaken for a straightforward endorsement of its male protagonist's desire to mold and possess the woman he obsessively loves—not after Judy's flashback, after the heartbreaking makeover scenes, after Johnny's terrifying murderous rage in the final scene, and so on. In general, how "personal" I assume an artwork to be actually factors little into my appreciation for most films I consider genuinely great; it just doesn't seem a valid criterion. The opposite is true for Wiseau. This tells me that, to truly love a film for being "so bad it's good," I must believe it to be not only a failure but a peculiarly *passionate failure* (to quote Susan Sontag on camp).[4] I assume that it allows me to watch an (incompetent) artist reveal their deepest selves transparently (though largely unwittingly) through their art. In other words, when appreciating a film like this, in some strange way, I allow myself to become a wholesale Romantic.

And perhaps it's this above all that appeals to me about a film like *The Room*. This is one of the only areas of contemporary culture where it feels appropriate to use concepts that we are often today justifiably wary of applying to most media: "authenticity," "sincerity"—perhaps even, in some perverse sense, "truth."[5] Indulging in this way of experiencing *The Room* requires that the artwork itself remain bad. But the aesthetic *experience* the artwork provides can nonetheless be all those things we've long hoped for from the artistic encounter: affecting, mesmerizing, cathartic—in short, so, so good.

JAMES MACDOWELL is Associate Professor of Film and Television Studies at the University of Warwick. He is author of *Irony in Film* and *Happy Endings in Hollywood Cinema: Cliché, Convention and the Final Couple.*

Notes

1. *Vertigo*'s Johnny is also known by the nickname Scottie.
2. See, for example, Wood, *Hitchcock's Films Revisited*; Modleski, *Women Who Knew Too Much*.
3. I have worked through this argument about *The Room* at greater length in an article cowritten with James Zborowski, "The Aesthetics of 'So Bad It's Good.'" For a complementary, more explicitly philosophical approach, you might read Dyck and Johnson, "Appreciating Bad Art," 279–92.
4. Sontag, "Notes on 'Camp,'" 275–92.
5. For a good discussion of this, see Pavlounis, "Sincerely Celebrating Failure."

5 EVERYBODY BETRAY ME!

REVENGE, REVERSE REVENGE, AND SLAVE MORALITY IN THE ROOM

JOHN DYCK

The Room is so funny, and so bizarre, that it's easy to miss how dismal the film is. This is embarrassing, but I only recently realized that the story is at its heart a tragedy: Johnny, the protagonist, is betrayed by both his fiancée and his best friend, and this betrayal leads him to suicide. *The Room* may crisscross several other genres, too, but they are all grim. It's partially a romantic film, but the romance fails. It's partially about a bromance between Johnny and Mark, but the friendship does not survive. The formal aspects of the film are no less bleak. The shots are often shadowy and dark, and nearly all of the film's instrumental score is in a minor key. (The only exceptions are the songs—all played during sex scenes, and nearly all in major keys.)

The climax of Johnny's suicide makes the film especially tragic. If the film's problem is how Johnny ought to respond to his betrayal, suicide is its solution. Having scrutinized the film at length, I believe that its fundamental conceit is to vindicate Johnny in the face of betrayal. If that's right, suicide is a form of revenge: Lisa and Mark have wronged Johnny by their trysts, and suicide is Johnny's way to get even. In the final scene, Mark leaves Lisa, disgusted by his own betrayal of his best friend. Sobbing, Lisa admits her mistake. Lisa and Denny are left weeping over Johnny's dead body. Johnny's suicide inflicts pain—and a painful revelation—on both Lisa and Mark; it's through the suicide that they finally admit their wrongdoing. But it also damns them because they are in some way responsible for Johnny's death. In other words, *The Room* is a revenge fantasy. Like all revenge fantasies, it plays out the sadistic inclinations of its protagonist. Johnny gets even with those who have wronged him.

Revenge versus Reverse Revenge

If it's a revenge fantasy, though, *The Room* isn't typical. Revenge fantasies usually involve physical retribution. In *Taken*, Liam Neeson's character takes out his daughter's kidnappers. In the first *John Wick* movie, Keanu Reeves's character is a methodical angel of death, meting out revenge on his puppy's killers. Revenge in *The Room* is psychological, not physical. Johnny isn't inflicting bodily harm on anyone. The ruination he brings is emotional and moral.

Additionally, revenge fantasies usually involve the protagonist's victory. But there is no such victory in *The Room*; Johnny not only commits suicide but also suffers injustice and humiliation throughout the film. I will argue, however, that there's a good reason for this: in addition to being a revenge fantasy, *The Room* is also a reverse revenge fantasy, for the protagonist also faces revenge or punishment. The story is thus a masochistic projection of Johnny's own suffering. Of course, the overall story line is meant to vindicate Johnny as an ideal lover and to excoriate Lisa for her unfaithfulness to him. But for this to work, we need to see that Johnny is a selfless martyr deserving of our sympathy. So the film goes out of its way to illustrate how much Johnny endures in his relationships. He gives himself to those who take advantage of his good nature, suffering constant pain, humiliation, and rejection from those close to him—not just from Lisa and Mark, but even from his other friends. In fact, the closer someone is to Johnny, the more fractured their relationship with him is.

I'm borrowing the idea of a reverse revenge fantasy from an essay by Christopher Rodkey about *God's Not Dead,* another classic of the so-bad-it's-good genre.[1] *God's Not Dead* centers on a college student who takes an introductory philosophy class. On the first day of class, the philosophy professor demands that all of the students pledge fealty to atheism. Our hero, however, refuses to deny his Christian faith, and in response his professor insists they debate the truth of theism in class. Rodkey argues that the film functions as a reverse revenge fantasy for evangelical Christians: it plays out their fears that they are being persecuted and mistreated. Though the story depicted in the film might be purely fictitious, it helps its evangelical audience believe that they, as Christians, are being persecuted—that universities are strongholds of anti-Christian propaganda, dedicated to causing Christians to suffer. (Subsequent films in the franchise also cater to these concerns. In a sequel, another protagonist, a high school teacher, finds herself in trouble with the law after merely referring to a quotation by Jesus.)

Superficially, *The Room* and *God's Not Dead* couldn't be more different, but closer inspection reveals a deep similarity in theme. Used and abused by those around him—at least as *The Room*'s creator, Tommy Wiseau, would have it—Johnny has no choice but to commit suicide, damning all those close to him who drove him to his desperate final act. What makes this even more fascinating is how, in its reverse revenge fantasy structuring, *The Room* inadvertently (I think) becomes a prime example of Nietzschean slave morality. To see this, though, we need to first identify a pattern in Johnny's relationships.

Circles of Friendship in *The Room*

The Room is a movie about relationships. Specifically, it's about Johnny's relationships as he alternates in the roles of best friend, romantic lover, father figure, and so on. We can think of three levels of attachment in the film, listed here in increasing degrees of intimacy: formal acquaintances, friends, and lovers/best friends. When we look at these relationships, we see a pattern: the closer people get to Johnny, the more fraught their bonds are.

The outer circle consists of formal acquaintances, the people Johnny interacts with regularly but not intimately. This circle includes the florist and the barista. The film goes out of its way to show that Johnny is on great terms with the people he sees regularly but isn't friends with. Remember how the florist tells Johnny that he's her favorite customer? Johnny is also on good terms with the barista, Susan, when he meets Mark at the coffee shop. Johnny treats these people well, and they treat him well.

The middle circle consists of Johnny's friends or buddies. Johnny's friends are other men, and their interactions involve bits of prototypical masculinity—throwing a football around, commenting on women. But there are very few scenes with Johnny and his friends that aren't fraught. Most of these scenes involve tension and argument, and even teasing or injury. Johnny's friends, for example, are constantly taunting one another ("cheep, cheep, cheep!"). There are four scenes where Johnny and his friends throw a football around; in all but one of them, someone gets hurt by falling down, and every time, the hurt person expresses frustration while dark music plays. Mike and Michelle even use Johnny's house as a place to hook up, suggesting a lack of respect for his intimate space. Peter always plays the psychologist, never the friend.

Even Denny, perhaps the purest character in the movie (apart from Johnny, of course), causes Johnny pain. Denny confesses to him that he's in love with Lisa, a moment foreshadowed by Denny's attempt to watch Johnny and Lisa have sex. Denny is enacting his own kind of betrayal of Johnny, even though Johnny has basically adopted him. When

Denny confesses his love for Lisa, Johnny's trusting nature comes to the fore. We are made to understand that Johnny will do everything for his friends, even as they betray him.

But Johnny suffers most from those in the inner circle, those closest to him: Lisa and Mark. It's striking that throughout the entire movie Lisa and Johnny share very few tender moments. Sex scenes are nearly the only times in which Johnny and Lisa's relationship is not tainted by fighting or guile.

The film blames Lisa, much more than Mark, for their betrayal. Whereas Mark is constantly tormented by the fact that he's betraying his best friend, Lisa actively seduces Mark. She is eager to betray Johnny, but Mark does so reluctantly, only as a result of being seduced. She is tearing Johnny apart—causing emotional pain, driving him to alcohol, and so on. (Both Lisa's mother, Claudette, and her friend Michelle try to convince Lisa that she is making a mistake by cheating on Johnny, to no avail. "You have to live, live, live," she icily tells Michelle.) There's more evidence here for the relationship between a character's closeness to Johnny and the degree of pain they cause him. While Mark may be Johnny's best male (i.e., platonic) friend, Lisa is supposed to be his *true* best friend, his life partner, his future wife. And thus she is the most destructive of all.

But Mark is no innocent bystander, either. In various scenes with Johnny, he acts deviously, making vague mentions of the woman he's seeing. In the world of the film, Mark and Lisa are morally bad—they are evil.

What should we make of the fact that the more involved people are with Johnny, the more hostility he experiences from them? One reading is that something about Johnny causes those close to him to betray him. But this is obviously not the film's logic. If we follow this line of thought, we'll conclude that Johnny is a bad person—he must be, if people close to him are always betraying him. This conclusion is absurd.

Instead, these concentric circles work to vindicate Johnny in a complicated way. Narratively, the film faces a problem it must resolve: if Johnny suffers at the hands of his friends, he needs to be justified. The audience needs to know that Johnny is a good person and doesn't deserve his mistreatment. And Johnny's relationships are what justify him. Acquaintances at the outer circle show that Johnny's mistreatment is not due to any failing of his own. Johnny's interactions with ordinary people show that impartial observers recognize Johnny's outstanding personality—his good qualities—and treat him well as a result. Johnny's circle of friends, however, mistreat him, abusing these very qualities. Johnny doesn't suffer because he deserves it; he suffers because his friends are bad people. The film constantly reinforces just how good Johnny is to his close friends.

As I've argued, one of the main goals of the film is to portray Johnny's undeserved suffering at the hands of those around him, especially those closest to him. In this way, *The Room* is a reverse revenge fantasy. Johnny suffers because of his care for others. But how do we reconcile this reverse revenge fantasy with the film's revenge fantasy? How do we make sense of the fact that Johnny suffers at the hands of his friends yet also gets revenge through his suicide? To explain this, we will turn to Nietzsche.

Slave Morality in *The Room*

The Room is a morality story. But unlike traditional morality tales, it does not try to show that morality leads to wealth, happiness, or some other ostensibly positive outcome. In the world of *The Room,* the righteous

5.1 Denny mourns Johnny. © 2003 by Wiseau-Films. (Movie still from *The Room*.)

suffer for their righteousness. Johnny is vindicated, but his vindication is purely moral—Johnny doesn't enjoy any material benefits from being a good person. After all, he dies at the end. Johnny reminds me of Christ on Good Friday: suffering alone, abandoned by his friends, and betrayed. His death, in the end, causes his friends to see how blind they were and how much they took for granted. Wiseau could have chosen many ways to vindicate Johnny in the face of his betrayal; the fact that he is vindicated through suicide is significant. It's what makes the film strikingly tragic.

Johnny also suffers in many other ways throughout the film. His care for his friends is often portrayed as sacrificial and kind, and his friends take advantage of these sacrifices. Johnny works hard to care for Lisa. He is attentive to her needs, which include sex (he checks to make sure she enjoys it); clothing (he buys her a sexy red dress); flowers; and so on. Remember Claudette's defense of Johnny: "He bought you a car. He bought you a ring, clothes, whatever you wanted. Now you want to dump him? That's not right." Others also cause him to suffer. Johnny has been wronged at work by not getting his promotion, despite working hard to secure big deals at the bank. Johnny takes care of Denny, even though Denny is in love with Lisa—and not shy about expressing his affection for her.

The film elicits our sympathy for Johnny in other ways than just his suffering. When Johnny tells the story of how he and Lisa met, the power differential between them is clear. He first meets her while he's working as a busser at a coffee shop. Then, on their first date, he explains, "She paid for dinner." It doesn't seem right to read this as an expression of Johnny's feminism or advocacy for equality, especially given all of the masculine tropes in the film. The point instead is likely to reinforce Johnny's status as poor, resilient, and hardworking, as someone worthy of pity.

This moral landscape is a striking demonstration of what Nietzsche says about traditional Christian morality in *On the Genealogy of Morality*. Before monotheism, Nietzsche argues, people used a "master" conception of morality: a good person was by definition someone who had wealth, a good life, and, above all, power. But, Nietzsche says, morality underwent a kind of reversal in ancient Near East thought. This reversal was initiated in early Judaism; it culminated in Jesus as the ultimate example. Influenced by the teachings of Jesus, people started employing a "slave" conception of morality: a good person suffered at the hands of others, lived for the good of others, and received no benefit for their work and suffering. In fact, the more oppressed you were—the more you suffered—the better you must be.

This is how Nietzsche illustrates the cry of slave morality, putting himself in the role of the enslaved: "Only those who suffer are good, only the poor, the powerless, the lowly are good; the suffering, the deprived, the sick, the ugly, are the only pious people, the only ones saved, salvation is for them alone, whereas you rich, the noble and powerful, you are eternally wicked, cruel, lustful, insatiate, godless, you will also be eternally wretched, cursed and damned!"[2]

According to slave morality, suffering makes one good—it allows oppressed people to feel vindicated and to feel psychologically superior. But, Nietzsche points out, the superiority is purely psychological; it has no material benefits and is merely "imaginary revenge."[3] In fact, it has significant material costs as the oppressed people lean into their suffering, since suffering is exactly what offers moral redemption. To bring this back to *The Room*, Johnny's selfless care of others is exactly what justifies him—and what causes others to take advantage of him.

Slave morality grows out of what Nietzsche calls "ressentiment"—oppressed peoples' resentment of their masters or bosses. In a slave morality framework, Christianity offers a unique way for slaves to deal with their own suffering. Instead of revolting, instead of really rejecting their masters, Nietzsche claims that these oppressed people create a system of morality that justifies them above their masters. But of course this causes no relief for the slaves; it only encourages their enslavement, as Nietzsche explains: "The beginning of the slaves' revolt in morality occurs when *ressentiment* itself turns creative and gives birth to values: the *ressentiment* of those beings who, denied the proper response of action, compensate for it only with imaginary revenge."[4]

The moral logic of *The Room* is slave morality. In the film's telling, Johnny is a good person precisely because of his suffering. This illuminates how *The Room* can be both a revenge fantasy and a reverse revenge fantasy. It's a revenge fantasy in a purely psychological, moral sense—a sense of slave morality. Yet because of Johnny's suicide, *The Room* is a reverse revenge fantasy in material terms. Thus if Johnny is to gain moral superiority, he must first suffer materially.

Johnny suffers precisely in his sacrifices, and those sacrifices are what vindicate his revenge. Yet the revenge is perfectly imaginary. Nietzsche himself couldn't have given a better example of how this logic plays out. *The Room* gives us a picture of how slave morality can exist not just in the general power struggles that make up society, as Nietzsche thought of it, but in intimate relationships with friends and lovers. The character of Johnny serves as an unintentional warning: don't make yourself the tragic figure of your own story. It's too narcissistic to think that others are always tearing us apart or to look for reasons to tear others apart. Instead of seeking to dole out revenge or receive it, we can move on. As Peter says, "Sometimes, life gets complicated. The unexpected can happen. When it does, you just gotta deal with it."

JOHN DYCK is Postdoctoral Teaching Fellow in Aesthetics and Philosophy at Auburn University. His work appears in *Journal of Aesthetics and Art Criticism* and *Journal of Value Inquiry.*

Notes

1. Christopher Rodkey, "*God's Not Dead* as Reverse Revenge Fantasy."
2. Nietzsche, *On the Genealogy of Morality*, 17.
3. Nietzsche, *On the Genealogy of Morality*, 20.
4. Nietzsche, *On the Genealogy of Morality*, 20.

6 ANYTHING FOR MY PRINCESS

USING DON QUIXOTE *TO BRING (SOME) COHERENCE TO* THE ROOM

ADAM M. ROSEN

One of the most interesting paradoxes of *The Room* is how it can feel so timelessly generic and utterly dated at the same time. In contrast, the most celebrated films are often inextricably tied to a particular age. *Easy Rider* (1969), *Escape from New York* (1981), and *Reality Bites* (1994), to offer just a few examples, all bring to mind specific historical moments, and as a result, they are often invoked as stand-ins for the zeitgeist of the eras in which they appeared. Even sci-fi or other nonrealist films that are meant as allegories—say, *They Live* (1988)—can be traced back to certain trends or events once their symbolism is unpacked (in the case of *They Live,* the supposed mindless consumerism of the 1980s). The same goes for less deliberately made or even "bad" films. Despite their shortcomings, they almost always give *some* indication of the time and place they're operating in, whether through their soundtrack, fashions, subject matter, or references to the outside world.

The Room, though, seems to exist in a temporal and contextual void. Throughout the entire film, there are almost no direct or even indirect mentions of real-life events, people, media, brands, or places. Even Mark and Johnny's coffee-shop outing, one of the few scenes filmed on location, feels off-kilter, with a tenuous connection to the real world. In what sort of universe does everyone at a hip urban coffee shop order cheesecake? Scrambling things further, the soundtrack, consisting as it does of over-the-top MTV-era R & B clichés, is a throwback to the mid-1990s and would have felt dated by the year of the movie's release, 2003. Ditto Denny's severe center part and rugby shirt—middle and high school fashions also decidedly of the 1990s.[1]

The film's San Francisco setting is repeatedly emphasized, yes, but interactions with the city are extremely superficial, made up of characters' brief forays into tourist hot spots (riding a trolley, running up a steep set of stairs with the bay in the background, tossing a football in Golden Gate Park) and of establishing shots—by their very nature generic and from a distance, hardly an ideal means for conveying the human-scale intimacy of a living, breathing place. It's a version of San Francisco that lives on a postcard or tourist brochure, glossy and iconic but totally unmoored to any moment in time or cultural context. *Taxi Driver* isn't a "New York movie" because the Empire State Building makes an appearance.

Most glaringly—and famously—the room where the majority of *The Room*'s scenes take place, the living area in Johnny and Lisa's home, is puzzlingly free of normal American household bric-a-brac, the not-so-useless clutter that usually serves as a tipoff to the viewer. There are no pictures of friends or family, no artwork or posters, no heaving stack of old newspapers and issues of *Time* magazine, no worn-down universal remote, no of-the-era furniture. There are, however, framed stock photos of spoons. The space has all the ambience of a cleaned-out Bed, Bath & Beyond showroom—which is to say, none. (For a deeper exploration of this space, see chapter 13.)

Given the film's frustrating lack of context clues, a different interpretive approach is needed to decode *The Room's* thematic setting: one that peels away the movie's bizarre and empty outer trappings to reveal its true essence. Using this approach, we end up in a similarly strange but much more defined place, one that gives (some) explanation as to where *The Room* is coming from.

The Power of Love

Thematically, *The Room* is a much older film than its mishmash of odd 1990s reference points and non sequiturs about "the computer business" suggest. In fact, its obsessive focus on romantic love, proper ways of being, and honor and shame signals that the movie hearkens back to a much earlier era: the age of chivalry. After viewing *The Room* several times, one gets the overwhelming sense that one is watching some sort of madcap modern twist on chivalric romances. This being the case, there is arguably no better guide for interpreting the film than *Don Quixote,* the ultimate madcap critique of this old but immortal genre. With every screening of *The Room,* Miguel de Cervantes is no doubt chuckling from the grave, consoled by the latest validation of his timeless work and the continued folly of humans, who, as *The Room* makes clear, appear to have learned little since *Don Quixote* was published in 1605.

This interpretation has the most purchase if we think of *The Room* as only a piece in the larger story of Wiseau's life, which of course it is. As has been documented, most extensively in *The Disaster Artist* book and film but in news articles, research, and documentaries as well, Wiseau has had a colorful—some might even say *quixotic*—life before and after the making of the movie. Hence, the *Don Quixote* interpretative framework applies on two interrelated levels: first, to Wiseau's quest to make an unforgettable film without any training, movie industry connections, acting talent, or filmmaking experience and, second, to Johnny's journey to discover Lisa's duplicity and learn the truth about the relationships with those he trusted. Indeed, these two "characters"—Johnny and Wiseau—are so intimately tied together that eventually they flatten into a single individual. Call him Johnny Wiseau.

Let's start with the most obvious similarities between Johnny (Wiseau) and Don Quixote. Physically, there's more than a passing resemblance between the hero of *The Room* and the hero of Cervantes's masterpiece, who "was fifty years old; his complexion weathered, his flesh scrawny, his face gaunt."[2] Such scruffy masculinity seems to just as easily describe Johnny (Wiseau); in *The Disaster Artist* book, Sestero approvingly recalls that "the best description I ever heard of Tommy was that he looks like one of the anonymous, Uzi-lugging goons who appeared for two seconds in a Jean-Claude Van Damme film before getting kicked off a catwalk."[3] Both men dress in a way that's meant to signal their alpha male status and toughness, but fail completely: Don Quixote wears old, rusted armor, with a helmet containing a jury-rigged pasteboard visor, and Johnny alternately sports frumpy oversized suits with a loose tie and sleeveless V-necks with warm-up pants, hardly the sort of attire the successful power yuppie he so obviously aspires to be would wear.

Both heroes speak with an uncanny tone and grammar that only makes sense to them. Don Quixote apes the conversational style of the over-the-top chivalric romances that have so enchanted him; every disagreement, no matter how petty, is treated as an outrageous insult to his dignity, and every woman he encounters, including those "of easy virtue," is treated as a "highborn maiden" to whom he pledges undying honor. Similarly, when Johnny isn't speaking in awkward clichés and odd, nearly nonsensical phrases, he is often indignant, even when such a harsh tone isn't warranted. "How dare you talk to me like that!" he scolds Lisa during one of their arguments. Additionally, despite their considerable verbal and physical eccentricities, both men have skeptical but loyal assistants who accompany them on their ultimately doomed sagas (Sancho Panza and Mark/Greg Sestero).

The origins of Don Quixote and Johnny (Wiseau) are also both mysterious. "Some claim that his family name was Quixada, or Quexada, for there is a certain amount of disagreement among the authors who wrote of this matter, although reliable conjecture seems to indicate that his name was Quexana," writes Cervantes,[4] in language familiar to anyone who has tried to uncover snatches of Wiseau's background. Some rumormongers have named his birthplace as various locations in eastern Europe, although Wiseau has always claimed he's from New Orleans.

The inspiration for the men's adventures is nearly identical. Don Quixote consumed histrionic books of chivalry for days and days, until "his brains began to [dry] up" and he came to believe that *he* was actually a knight-errant destined to right the world's wrongs (see fig. 6.1).[5] Not all too dissimilarly, by the time Wiseau wrote *The Room,* he had come to idolize iconic relationship dramas such as *A Streetcar Named Desire, Rebel Without a Cause,* and *The Talented Mr. Ripley,* and their all-American male leads, Marlon Brando, James Dean, and Matt Damon, respectively. He was, to use a favored term in *Don Quixote,* hopelessly *enchanted* by the movie screen. "And so it was that with these exceedingly agreeable thoughts, and carried away by the extraordinary pleasure he took in them, he hastened to put into effect what he so fervently desired,"[6] Cervantes writes, describing Tommy Wiseau—and all delusional dreamers—just as much as Don Quixote.

And, of course, there is the obsessive preoccupation with romance. From the very beginning of *The Room,* it's established that Johnny is a true believer when it comes to the art of seduction and love. "Hi, babe! I have something for you," he announces in the film's very first scene, entering the home he shares with Lisa while clutching a bouquet of red roses and a slinky red dress in a gift-wrapped box (see fig. 6.2). As any couple who has cohabited long term can surely attest, this is hardly typical weekday behavior. Johnny, however, is far from typical when

6.1 "Don Quixote Knighted by the Innkeeper." From *Don Quixote of the Mancha,* written by Judge Parry and illustrated by Walter Crane.

6.2 Johnny gifts Lisa a red dress. © 2003 by Wiseau-Films. (Movie still from *The Room*.)

it comes to love. "Anything for my princess," he coos, as Lisa twirls serenely in her new outfit. Just a few minutes later, the couple proceeds to have sex, and for several drawn-out minutes; it will be one of four such scenes with Lisa in the movie (two with Johnny and two with Mark). All of this, much like Don Quixote's constant, albeit failed, exhibitions of chivalric deeds, is meant to signal just how seriously Johnny/Wiseau believes in romantic love. After all, one does not simply include over ten minutes of soft-core sex in a movie if one isn't serious about such things.

Speaking of princesses, it's no coincidence that Johnny calls Lisa one in the scene described above. Whether Wiseau was conscious of it or not, this is obviously the classic language of chivalry. It is the language of putting women on pedestals, much as a medieval romance novel would. For his own part, Don Quixote refers to the object of his affection, a peasant girl named Aldonza Lorenzo, as "Princess Dulcinea, mistress of this captive heart."[7] This is more than just a flight of fancy; the gap between his image of her and reality, much like Wiseau's perspective on his artistic achievement and the world's reception of it, epitomized "the measureless distance between the high purpose Don Quixote sets out to enact and the world as it is."[8]

My Favorite Customer in All the Land

All of these similarities hint at the endless connections between Don Quixote and Johnny/Wiseau. But arguably the biggest parallel between these characters lies in their social mission. Like Don Quixote, Johnny is obsessed with what he believes to be honorable human conduct. *The Room* is filled with explicit discussions of loyalty and faithfulness, betrayal and backstabbing. "I treat you like a princess and you stab me in the back," Johnny says to Lisa in their final scene together, just before his suicide—which, significantly, is triggered by Lisa, who is cast in the storybook role of the evil, unfaithful woman.

Just so the audience is completely clear on her guilt, after discovering Johnny's dead body, Mark spits at her, "Tramp! You killed him. You're the cause of all of this." Because Wiseau really wants to get his points across—and, perhaps, because he dislikes or lacks an understanding of subtext—these sorts of teachable moments are relentless in the film. In an earlier scene, possibly meant to foreshadow the revelation of Lisa's duplicity, Johnny insists to Mark, "I don't have to worry

. . . because Lisa is loyal to me." This on-the-nose declaration is typical of the film's didactic approach. Indeed, Mark is described as Johnny's "best friend" no less than seven times in the movie, in case we forget just how close their bond is and just how much weight his betrayal is meant to carry.

Whatever its shortcomings from a narrative perspective, all this clumsy exposition makes the film feel like an over-the-top morality tale—because it is. "*The Room* teaches you what not to do to be a better person," Wiseau asserts in the DVD's commentary, in a delicious bit of Quixotian irony. How right he is.[9]

Over-the-top moralizing was the exact sort of thing *Don Quixote* intended to poke fun at. And Cervantes had lots of material to work with. According to scholars Durán and Rogg, "Cervantes's novel can be placed historically between two great waves of didactic-moralizing literature, the first in medieval times anchored in Christian morality and the second during the Counter-Reformation as a reaction against Renaissance uncertainty or skepticism."[10] Don Quixote's biggest targets, such as the fictional heroes Don Belianís of Greece, Orlando Furioso, and Amadís of Gaul, were part of this first wave, created to instruct (and entertain) their audiences in proper behavior in love and life. *Don Quixote* was a reaction to them.

Don Quixote's multiple stories within a story, long-winded tales about lovers scorned and betrayed (many by supposed best friends, to boot), highlight the tedium and repetitiveness of chivalric tropes. But more important, and more lasting, is the way the book exposes the vanity of Don Quixote's extravagant sense of righteousness. In a fake sonnet dedicated to Don Quixote at the beginning of the book, Don Belianís writes, "And yet, though my good fortunes ever soared / as high as the horned moon that sails the sky / I envy, O Quixote, your great feats!"[11] Orlando Furioso adds, "I cannot be your equal; I am humbled / by your prowess, your noble deeds, your fame."[12] These tributes to the greatness of Don Quixote are essentially the early seventeenth-century version of "Johnny wanted to adopt Denny. It's really a tragedy how many kids out there don't have parents. When Denny turned eighteen, Johnny found him a little apartment here in this building and he's paying for it until he graduates from school." *Behold Johnny's noble deeds, dear viewer,* Wiseau seems to be instructing us. *He is practically a modern-day knight.* Not only does he sponsor teenage orphans, but he is also a loyal husband, a wealthy man, a good provider (notwithstanding his lost promotion), a serious romantic, a friend to many, and a pillar of the community, highly respected by even the lowborn (flower shop owners, baristas, etc.).

That said, while it's easy to laugh at Johnny/Wiseau and *Don Quixote* for such shameless self-regard, maybe they're simply exaggerated versions of ourselves—we're just more subtle when it comes to personal mythmaking. To offer one current example, think about the infinite daily posts on social media in which someone mentions a kindness they recently performed or an outrage they're opposed to. Many of these posts go viral, yielding thousands of likes and showering attention on the poster. While the gestures may be commendable, a cynic might point out how much effort is involved, how eager these public do-gooders are for others to know about their deeds. As Lisa might say, "I told you, Mom, [Twitter handle *x*] is very caring about the people in their life."

Whether subtle or stealthy, though, didactic moralizing isn't limited to calculating social media users and makers of bad movies. By some lights, it never actually left the field of letters. In a recent essay whose findings would be recognizable to Cervantes, literary critic Becca Rothfeld provocatively diagnoses much of contemporary literary fiction as "sanctimony literature": writing that "is full of self-promotion and the airing of performatively righteous opinions. It exists largely to make poster-cum-authors look good and scrollers-cum-readers feel good for appreciating the poster-cum authors' goodness."[13] "These books—millennial agit-prop, millennial middlebrow—are inflated and animated by an unshakeable faith in their own rectitude," she writes.[14] Sound familiar?

The Once and Future Wife

Because of the unrelenting irony deployed in *Don Quixote* and the unrelenting sincerity in *The Room*, it's tempting to assume that for all their similarities, the works are ultimately irreconcilable. The dichotomies are obvious. Both result in a timeless farce, but they get there by opposite paths: *Don Quixote* is the creation of a man with acute observational powers and self-awareness, whereas *The Room* is the opposite. The setting of *Don Quixote* is extremely specific to a certain era, while *The Room* exists in a near void. And *Don Quixote* is intentional, while *The Room* does not at all seem to be, despite what Wiseau claims.

Be that as it may, the two are inextricably linked in two critical ways. The first is their personal connections to their protagonists. *Don Quixote* was a labor of love and a strenuous effort of its own, with much of the book drawn from Cervantes's adventure-filled and often penury-soaked life, just as *The Room* is widely believed to be drawn from Wiseau's own colorful exploits. Cervantes—who, it's worth mentioning, was a lover of chivalric romances[15]—was arguably just as much a character in his magnum opus, if much more subtly than Wiseau. He was so intertwined, in fact, that Don Quixote cannot fully be understood without accounting for him, insists Walter Starkie, one of several English translators of the book: "*Don Quixote* is one of those rare novels in which both the hero and the author are so closely related that it is not possible to study them apart. Just as Don Quixote was the reflection of the man Cervantes, so it is only in the record of the life of the latter that we may find the true interpretation of the Knight of the Rueful Figure."[16] As in *The Room,* the line where the author ends and the main character begins is so blurry the distinction essentially collapses.

The second crucial connection is that timelessness. The themes tackled in *The Room,* as distorted as they appear through the bizarro lens of Wiseau, were present at the time of Cervantes and will continue to exist so long as love is won and lost, best friends betray each other, and grown men call each other chicken. Timelessness suspends a work, allowing for all sorts of meanings to be projected on it depending on the current circumstances. "Through a re-casting of his glorious acts of heroism (or his comic misadventures) . . . he has been employed both as a Romantic hero and as a foolish, anachronistic madman, for the purposes of representing either high idealism or utter insanity, and sometimes both,"[17] wrote Robert Bayliss about Don Quixote, in words that apply just as well to any other weathered, overly sincere misfit.

ADAM M. ROSEN is a book editor and writer in Asheville, North Carolina, and a former associate editor in the Reference Division of Oxford University Press. He has contributed to the *Atlantic*.com, the *Los Angeles Review of Books,* the *Baltimore Sun,* the *Onion,* and many other print and online outlets.

Notes

1. According to *The Disaster Artist,* the actor who played Denny, Philip Haldiman, was twenty-six when the movie was filmed, making him older than Greg Sestero (Mark)—thus the attempt to turn him into an eighteen-year-old via hair part and rugby shirt. This was an interesting casting choice considering Mark is the best friend

(and thus presumably a peer) of Johnny, who is presented as old enough to be Denny's father.

2. Cervantes, *Don Quixote*, trans. Grossman, 18.
3. Sestero and Bissell, *Disaster Artist*, 26.
4. Cervantes, *Don Quixote*, trans. Grossman, 20.
5. Cervantes, *Don Quixote*, trans. Grossman, 21.
6. Cervantes, *Don Quixote*, trans. Grossman, 22.
7. Cervantes, *Don Quixote*, trans. Grossman, 25.
8. Holmes, "Don Quixote and Modern Man," 44.
9. Wiseau, "Interview with Tommy Wiseau."
10. Durán and Rogg, "Constructing Don Quixote," 66.
11. Cervantes, *Don Quixote*, trans. Grossman, 14.
12. Cervantes, *Don Quixote*, trans. Grossman, 14.
13. Rothfeld, "Sanctimony Literature," 105.
14. Rothfeld, "Sanctimony Literature," 107.
15. Cervantes, *Don Quixote*, trans. Starkie, 27.
16. Cervantes, *Don Quixote*, trans. Starkie, 15.
17. Bayliss, "What Don Quixote Means (Today)," 383.

CRYPTO-WISEAULOGY 7

UNCOVERING STANLEY KUBRICK, JEWISHNESS, AND JUDAISM IN THE ROOM

NATHAN ABRAMS

In 2012, a remarkable film appeared. Titled *Room 237* (directed by Rodney Ascher), after the eponymous room in Stanley Kubrick's *The Shining* (1980), it was a deadpan documentary that deconstructed the horror movie from a variety of perspectives. Using a form of Talmudic and Midrashic exegesis, the movie purported to uncover whether Kubrick's film is about the genocide of the Native Americans, the Holocaust, faked NASA moon landings, or the Minotaur. Behind this exercise lay the belief that the genius Stanley Kubrick had laced the film with hidden meanings. Some fans have canonized Kubrick as an "infallible perfectionist" with "overwhelming, God-like control and agency," whereby every ambiguity, continuity error, prop, and artistic decision is interpreted as a coded message and analyzed for hidden meaning.[1] There's no better example of this than Robert Shawn Montgomery, the proprietor of a website devoted to faithfully chronicling the connections between Kubrick films and major world events, who refers to his study as "Crypto-Kubrology."[2]

In this contribution, I ask what a similar movie about *The Room* might look like. Indulge me while we share a faith in the omniscient intentionality of *The Room*'s creator, in a mode like Kubrick's, to inquire, is there such a thing as Crypto-Wiseaulogy? As Greg Sestero, who costarred in the film, says, "No one interprets the world the way Tommy Wiseau does."[3] Let us, then, for a moment, consider Wiseau as a director whose genius lay in devising puzzles. In this vein, can we conceive of *The Room*, to paraphrase I. Q. Hunter, as resembling *The Da Vinci Code*, the viewer as Alan Turing confronted with an Enigma machine, and Wiseau as like Walter Sickert, who supposedly confessed in one of his East End paintings that he was Jack the Ripper?[4]

This may not be such a stretch as it first appears. Wiseau himself presents an obscure, curious image comparable to that of Kubrick, long perceived to be a private, elusive hermit. Like Kubrick—who transplanted himself to Britain in 1962—Wiseau is also an émigré, a stranger in a strange land. What do we know about the real Wiseau? What do we know about Kubrick? Wiseau, like Kubrick, has attracted a following that can be described as cultic. Perhaps even more so, for devotees turn up at midnight screenings, bring artifacts related to the film with them, engage in participatory rituals, and generally revel in the film's effect. Unlike with a Kubrick film, they may even be treated to an appearance of its creator in person, which brings an added frisson (Kubrick fans treat the rare footage of Kubrick at work, as seen in his daughter Vivian Kubrick's documentary *Making of "The Shining,"* with near sacrosanct status, believing it to be an unvarnished window into "the truth").

Another parallel also immediately presents itself. Kubrick's films did not fare well on their initial release, taking some ten or twenty years before earning critical acclaim; *2001: A Space Odyssey* (1968), *Barry Lyndon* (1975), *The Shining*, and *Eyes Wide Shut* (1999) all had a poor critical reception. In fact, *The Shining* had the worst reception of any major film in 1980, and it took some time for its critical reception to be revised. *The Room* similarly bombed at the box office when it was released, only to spawn a significant afterlife.

Like Kubrick, who was known for doing multiple takes until he was satisfied, Wiseau apparently had so many issues with the "I did not hit her" scene that it took a frustrating thirty-two takes before the crew got what they needed. This is even touched upon in James Franco's *The Disaster Artist*, where he recreates the failed attempts of Wiseau trying his hardest to make this scene work.

Just as the various interpretations in *Room 237* are held together by a belief that the film holds a secret message, so too is much of the criticism of *The Room*. As with Kubrick, fan forums obsess over the meaning of the film and attempt to deconstruct its discontinuities, as if they will turn up hidden meanings. As Greg Sestero points out in his book about the film, *The Disaster Artist*, this is a natural result of the movie's seeming incoherence: "Imagine a movie so incomprehensible that you find yourself compelled to watch it over and over again. You become desperate to learn how (if) on earth it was conceived: Who made it, and for what purpose?"[5]

Sestero continues, and it is worth citing him at length: "*The Room* is—despite its ostensibly simple plot—perhaps the most casually surreal film ever made. To put it simply, *The Room* doesn't work in any way films have evolved to work over the last century of filmmaking. It's filled with red herrings, shots of locations that are never visited, and entire conversations comprised of non sequiturs. It is, essentially, one gigantic plot hole. For many, experiencing *The Room* is both wildly exhilarating and supremely dislocating. The film engenders an obsessive fascination, instantly luring you into its odd, convoluted world."[6]

Although Wiseau, in Sestero's words, "is the key to *The Room*'s mystery," his opaque, elliptical, elusive, and uncommunicative nature means that the real job of interpretation is left up to us, the viewers.[7]

Let us begin with the title. In a special Q and A feature filmed for the DVD release, Wiseau explains that it is meant to evoke a safe place for viewers. However, is such an anodyne explanation adequate?

Clearly, on a simplistic level, the title refers to the space in which most of the action takes place—the front room of Johnny's apartment in San Francisco. An alternative suggestion, however, is that "the room" of the title is not an actual, physical space but a metaphorical one, referring to the interior space of Johnny's head. This would explain the innumerable discontinuities, inconsistencies, and lapses of logic in the plot; like a dream or memory, it does not need to make sense. Reinforcing this interpretation is the fact that Wiseau asked Juliette Danielle, who played Lisa, to watch and study Stanley Kubrick's final film, *Eyes Wide Shut*, which very much operates according to an oneiric dreamlike logic, for inspiration. This would also further explain the fake-looking nature of the apartment, which resembles a showroom in a catalog rather than a real, lived-in apartment. The DVD rack, for instance, only holds three DVDs. Dotted around are framed pictures of spoons. An incongruous fruit bowl sits on the coffee table. Other "exterior" settings, it turns out, are also completely mocked up for the film. This includes the alleyway and the rooftop, both of which were, in reality, located in a parking lot. The shots of real San Francisco, particularly Golden Gate Park, only serve to emphasize the falsity of these other locations.

Might we also appropriate Gilles Deleuze's formulation here, then, to say that the centerpiece room in the movie represents a brain?[8] The room and its environs, being so obviously fake, are external physical representations of Johnny's disordered mind and internal world. Its blatant anomalies and mistakes in layout translate into structural mind games in the film. In this way, the metaphysical space of the room invokes *The Shining*'s Overlook Hotel, which, as has been argued elsewhere, is not a literal construction but an allegorical representation of the disordered state of its protagonist's mind.[9] Cementing the connection is the name of *The Shining*'s protagonist (Jack), who also refers to himself as Johnny

7.1 Here's Johnny. © 1980 by Warner Bros. (Movie still from *The Shining*.)

(see fig. 7.1). Both Wiseau and Jack Nicholson, who played Jack in *The Shining*, produced over-the-top performances.

On the other hand, can we interpret *The Room* as being about making sense of the film itself, in that it is a meta-film about the movie's making in the way that *The Shining* has been interpreted as a meta-horror film? The room is a film set (as indeed it was), just like the Overlook Hotel. Johnny stands as a metonym for a writer-director losing control of his own cast and crew (and friends and family) while struggling to make his film, much as Jack fails to write his novel. Johnny is gradually driven to suicide, as Jack is driven to self-destruction.

Perhaps the most intriguing aspect of *The Room* involves its Jewishness. As with much of Kubrick's output, the plot of *The Room* is, on the surface, not at all Jewish. However, probe beneath its (celluloid) skin, and plenty of echoes and allusions emerge. To start, its very title invokes that of Jewish playwright Harold Pinter's titular 1957 play. As Ruby Cohn has pointed out in her 1962 essay "The World of Harold Pinter," "Pinter's rooms are stuffy, nonspecific cubes, whose atmosphere grows steadily more stale and more tense."[10] Such a description accurately describes *The Room*. In addition, Pinter populated his plays with such rooms. The titular room of his first play is "a room in a large house." In *The Dumb Waiter* (1957), we go down to "a basement room." *The Birthday Party* (1957) has a "living room of a house in a seaside town," and, in *The Caretaker* (1959), it is simply "a room." Cohn explains, "Pinter's rooms, parts of mysterious and infinite series, are like cells without a vista. At the opening curtain, these rooms look naturalistic, meaning no more than the eye can contain. But by the end of each play, they become sealed containers, virtual coffins. Within each Pinter room, the props seem to be realistically functional, and only in retrospect do they acquire symbolic significance."[11] Again, this description—particularly the parts referring to "realistically functional" props that acquire significance only in retrospect and to the room becoming a "coffin"—fits *The Room* perfectly.

The Room, much like *The Shining*, has important biblical resonances. Both lead characters are named Johnny, which can be read as a synonym for Jack, which is short for Jacob (*Ya'acov*), the biblical patriarch, whose sons are the ancestors of the twelve tribes of Israel. Jacob, son of Isaac, cheats his brother, Esau, out of his birthright by fooling their blind father. Nonetheless, he becomes the father of *B'nei Yisrael* ("Children of Israel") after his name is changed from *Ya'acov* to *Yisrael* ("Israel") following his struggle with the angel. Going back to the film, Jack, like Johnny in *The Room*, offers further biblical echoes in that they are the film's scapegoats, their sacrificial victims.

As with *The Shining*, numbers are important to *The Room*. Geoffrey Cocks has parsed the repeated use of sevens and multiples of seven, especially forty-two, in *The Shining*.[12] Seven is a number rich in symbolism in Judaism, and Cocks argues that forty-two refers to the year of the implementation of the Nazi genocidal program, the final solution. A similar numeric exercise can be undertaken with *The Room*. At one point, it is revealed that Johnny and Lisa have been together for five years; later it becomes seven. (Which is it? The actual number is perhaps unimportant because the whole story, and hence its details, are allegorical.) From a kabbalistic angle, such numbers become key, for both five and seven have profound significance including the five Books of the Torah and how seven is associated with, among many other things, God. The number four also punctuates the film: consider the number of letters in the word *room*, or the four separate music tracks listed in the film's credits, or its four main characters—Johnny, Lisa, Mark, and Denny. In addition, a football appears in four of the film's scenes, during which the male characters play catch among themselves. The recurrence of these *fours* in the film (echoing Kubrick's *2001: A Space Odyssey*, which is peppered with fours) invokes the Judaic approach known as *PaRDeS*, which seeks to penetrate a text through four layers of seeing. *PaRDeS* is an acronym for *Peshat* ("plain," "simple"); *Remez* ("hint"); *Derash* ("to inquire," "to seek"); and *Sod* ("secret," "mystery").[13]

Continuing the Jewish theme, pictures of spoons are dotted around the apartment. As a result, spoons have become a symbol attached to the film, and viewers take spoons to screenings and then throw them in the auditorium while watching the film. Spoons have biblical cultic significance because they were used in Temple worship.

The film also contains characters named Mark, Mike, Peter, and Steven. Is Johnny then some sort of Jesus-like figure who, spoiler alert, is martyred for our sins? As Greg Sestero relates it, Wiseau made his character "the one spotless human being amid chaos, lies, and infidelity. Johnny was perfect. He was a lost innocent, a pure victim."[14] Wiseau presents Johnny as the undeserving victim of all those around him: "Everybody betray me!" he exclaims in anguish. Certainly, his death has resonances of the Gospels, with his final cry, "God, forgive me" (although exactly what he needs to be forgiven for is never made clear). While this motif is seemingly more Christian than Jewish, recall that Jesus and the early apostles were all Jewish.

Again, *Eyes Wide Shut* may offer a clue. As mentioned above, Wiseau asked Juliette Danielle to watch and study the film for inspiration. Like Kubrick, he did not explain his reasons, but perhaps its reflection on marriage, jealousy, and sexual infidelity matched the themes of *The Room*. It's certainly worth pointing out, though, that *Eyes Wide Shut* is based on Jewish author Arthur Schnitzler's novella *Traumnovelle* (1926). Like its source, the film is "*echt* Jewish"; the Jewish traces remain despite the superficial whitewashing by Kubrick.[15] Likewise, in its vanilla Americanness, so too has *The Room* been scrubbed clean although it retains a residual Jewishness.

Maybe the film's Jewish resonances reside in Wiseau's extraordinary otherness. Wiseau is certainly an outsider, a loner, and a wanderer whose origins appear to be in eastern Europe via France, although no one is entirely certain because his ancestry is never clearly ascertained or confirmed. Jewish actor James Franco certainly perceived something resonant in Wiseau's background, given that he cast himself in the role of Tommy (and worked with a host of other Jewish actors). Adding to the mystery is Wiseau's refusal to reveal both the funding source of the film and his exact name—as Sestero relates, "Thomas P. Wiseau" is a change from his original legal name (and what does the P stand for?). In this way, he stands as a living metonym of those early Jewish pioneers who, on arriving in America, changed their names and who went on to develop the Hollywood studio system. Jews in early Hollywood became American by building and projecting a kind of fantasy America into which Americans then bought. Wiseau appears to have done the same.

Sestero informs us that "Tommy Wiseau intended *The Room* to be a serious American drama, a cautionary tale about love and friendship."[16] Consequently, Wiseau then projects onto Sestero an idealized version of American youth—and in the film, Wiseau's character seems to be a romanticized version of a great all-American guy (especially in the football scenes). In addition, as Sestero tells it, "Johnny's story was the perfect American drama—in Tommy's mind anyway."[17] Like the Jewish pioneers in Hollywood, Tommy sees promise in America, a place where he can make a $6 million film funded entirely from his own pocket. However, both Tommy and his fictional counterpart, Johnny, exude a sense of desperation and desire to be American. Both take on all the trappings of American life (football and so on) but never succeed in losing their otherness. In comparison to Wiseau/Johnny, those early generations of Jews who built Hollywood were more "successful" in effacing their Jewishness. By contrast, Wiseau cannot shed his outsider status and hence fails to "pass" as American.[18]

What is more, the wandering and the obscure origins all buy into Jewish stereotypes. Wiseau even suggests that he was a vampire and considered revealing himself as such in the film. This explains the sunglasses, pale skin, and lack of even basic football knowledge. Sestero adds that Johnny is possibly extraterrestrial. Both images have attached themselves to Jews over the years, from Bram Stoker's *Dracula* (1897) through to the extraordinary book *Les Juifs de l'espace/The Lost Tribes from Outer Space* (1974) by Marc Dem, in which he argues—seriously—that Jews come from space and will one day return there. Compounding this, that Johnny is a banker draws upon the age-old connection between Jews and money as personified by Shylock and Fagin. That Lisa is blonde, and hence representative of the archetypal shiksa goddess, also plays into Jewish visual tropes.

Here, I have argued that Jewishness and Judaism are the most important key to unlocking the secrets of *The Room*. I have made a similar argument about *The Shining*, one of the most well-known cult films of today. Is it possible that *The Room* will take its place alongside it? The evidence will lie in whether this current volume will be the first in a line of books devoted to this much-dismissed failure and whether, as I have suggested in this thought exercise, *The Room* will spawn its own version of *Room 237*.

NATHAN ABRAMS is Professor of Film at Bangor University. He is author of *Stanley Kubrick: New York Jewish Intellectual* and (with Robert P. Kolker) of *Eyes Wide Shut: Stanley Kubrick and the Making of His Final Film*.

Notes

1. Donnelly, *Shining*, 16.
2. Montgomery, "Cryptokubrology."
3. Sestero and Bissell, *Disaster Artist*, xv.
4. Hunter, *Cult Film as a Guide to Life*, 43.
5. Sestero and Bissell, *Disaster Artist*, xiii.
6. Sestero and Bissell, *Disaster Artist*.

7. Sestero and Bissell, *Disaster Artist*, xv.
8. Deleuze, *Cinema II*, 198.
9. See Abrams, *Stanley Kubrick*, 195–96.
10. Cohn, "World of Harold Pinter," 56.
11. Cohn, "World of Harold Pinter."
12. Cocks, *Wolf at the Door*.
13. See Abrams, *Stanley Kubrick*, 127.
14. Sestero and Bissell, *Disaster Artist*, 228.
15. See Kolker and Abrams, *Eyes Wide Shut*, 48.
16. Sestero and Bissell, *Disaster Artist*, xiii.
17. Sestero and Bissell, *Disaster Artist*, 228.
18. I am grateful to Keith Kahn-Harris for this observation.

PART III
CULT AND THE (CLASS)*ROOM*

I JUST LIKE TO WATCH YOU GUYS 8

HOW SCREENINGS OF THE ROOM *GIVE PEOPLE PERMISSION TO PERFORM*

ELLEN WRIGHT

I'm not going to lie. I'm a fraud. I only came to *The Room* five years ago, when I started my first permanent job as a lecturer in cinema history and was asked to redesign and deliver an existing undergraduate module that examined the phenomenon of cult film.

The Room was one of the few films on the existing module screening list that I hadn't seen. This is perhaps not surprising; to my knowledge, it has never been given a proper theatrical release here in the UK, nor can you buy it as a British DVD. But the title didn't ring a bell, even though I did my PhD alongside fan scholar Richard McCulloch, who was doing some fantastic research into the film and its admirers.[1]

My work colleague lent me his copy of the film, and I naively sat down to watch, on my sofa, on my own. What a mistake. Approaching *The Room* straight and unaccompanied was a real rookie move. I made it to the first excruciating sex scene and then had to take a break and do some other stuff. I went back and tried to watch again. I mean, how hard can it be to watch a film? I've got a doctorate in them! I've had to watch all manner of art cinema nonsense over the years. This shouldn't have been an issue. But with each minute of viewing, my tolerance levels got worse. I found myself only able to watch in ten-to-fifteen-minute bursts and became frustrated. I rapidly realized there was no way I could screen this on my undergraduate module. My end-of-term student feedback would be awful.

It was only then, I'm ashamed to say, that it dawned on me: I was watching the film all wrong. Despite also proposing to screen *The Rocky Horror Picture Show* on the module and deciding to talk about whether or not *Mamma Mia!* qualifies as a legitimate cult text (both films known for their fervent audience followings and the enthusiastic interactions they can prompt at screenings), I hadn't considered the broader reception context of *The Room*—namely, its audience and the spaces in which one might consume such a film, arguably the most important element in the making of a cult text. Cult audiences do not consume the objects of their affection in a "typical" way. Just as a religious cult can be termed "a community, a commonality of congregation that sees itself at odds with normalised culture," as cult film scholars Mathijs and Sexton observe, the same goes for a cult film audience.[2] Rather than embarking on the usual Western cinema-going experience of isolated, concentrated, and quiet engagement, cult audiences engage much more actively with their object of reverence, instead treating screenings as a social, collective, almost tribal experience frequently characterized by ritualized behaviors and voluble, sometimes physical interactions with fellow audience members and the films themselves.

I turned to McCulloch's work, which talked about the considerable creativity attendees demonstrated when responding to *The Room* at screenings at London's repertory cinema, the Prince Charles Cinema, and the camaraderie, the commitment, and the genuine affection it engendered for this genuinely bad film. Suddenly a light came on. I had a new appreciation for the film and its audience. I bought and devoured Greg Sestero and Tom Bissell's book about the making of the movie, *The Disaster Artist*, and learned about a film adaptation that was hopefully coming in the future. I went, with friends, to the Prince Charles for a late-night screening that included a Q and A with Sestero and Tommy Wiseau, and we had a ball.

This seemed like an ideal opportunity for engaging with my long-standing fascination with film and theater audiences and their behavior. During my own time as a student, I worked in cabaret to pull in some extra money. I produced and hosted a regular burlesque show, and I loved it. I loved how fun and bawdy it was, how people dressed up and got involved, how I could say the filthiest, most unladylike things on stage and the audience ate it up. In that space I wasn't everyday me, nor was anyone else. We were given permission to perform, play, and be outrageous. The screening at the Prince Charles had the same vibe. I felt as if I had come home. *The Room* went from being the turkey I would have to ditch from my module to the jewel in the crown.

(For what it's worth, working in cabaret gave me fantastic training for being a lecturer. If you have the skills to hold 250 drunken, paying punters in the palm of your hand, then lecturing to seventy students is a walk in the park—provided you remember to hold back on the salty stories and language! You learn how to engage people directly and meaningfully and, perhaps more importantly, how best to use your space.)

As I've already mentioned, elsewhere on the module I was proposing to show *The Rocky Horror Picture Show,* but without any of the participatory elements. I am lucky enough to teach and screen films in a working independent art cinema. Accordingly, I couldn't endorse toilet rolls and toast flying about, or squirting water pistols and the like. In addition, my screenings normally take place around 11:00 a.m., and I couldn't imagine the students turning up in the city-center cinema dressed as Dr. Frank-N-Furter or Riff Raff.

However, *The Room could* provide an alternative, and possibly less embarrassing or involved, opportunity for the students to enter a much-needed space in which they could become immersed, to *play at* and with being a cult audience, to perform, participate, and *have fun*. Through *The Room*, they could experience firsthand some of the ideas of ownership, belonging, and rebellion that so many cult communities exemplify and espouse and that I wanted so badly for them to understand and appreciate so they stand the best chance of passing their assessed assignments. I wasn't interested in how technically bad the film was, and I didn't want the students to focus on that either. I wanted them to think about what pleasures an audience might feasibly get out of going to a screening of *The Room*.

Film scholar Richard Dyer has talked about entertainment as being utopian "wish-fulfilment" and "something better to escape into or something we want deeply that our everyday lives don't provide,"[3] a form that purposely generates positive feelings in its audience. He talks about Hollywood musicals (a film genre that has fostered many an enthusiastic cult following) as the epitome of entertainment, and just as performers in musicals have no issue with spontaneously launching into enthusiastic song-and-dance sequences in the most improbable of circumstances, I want my students to see the potential in the lecture hall (or in my case the cinema auditorium). It need not be a dimly-lit, dry, and essentially still space where they can furtively nurse last night's hangover, catch a quiet nap, or simply let the learning wash over them; it could be a demanding, stimulating participatory space full of shadowy, enticing, and undiscovered corners that actively encourages the audience to spontaneously explore and express themselves and maybe—just maybe—even have fun.

Obviously, this screening would essentially be what French philosopher Jean Baudrillard would call a "simulacrum," or an imitation, rather than the genuine experience one would get at a cinema such as the Prince Charles, but weren't those "authentic" screenings performances too? A ritual of sorts where certain behaviors have become expected?

The Room was to be the final screening on the module, which ends at Christmas, so this screening was sold to my students as the end-of-term reward for their hard work and engagement. They were encouraged to Google the "best worst film ever" in advance and learn a bit about the film's context so they wouldn't make my mistake of coming to the film dry. I printed out and distributed a one-page "Participants' Guide to *The Room*" cheat sheet with a few quick and easy callouts and behaviors that the students could have a go at, should they want to. I bought two inflatable American footballs, which I gave to two particularly enthusiastic students, and five hundred plastic spoons, which I shared out. The projectionist turned down the lights, and off we went.

In October 2020 I'll be running this module for the fifth year, and I'm confident it will be a blast for students, as always. Every time *The Room* screening has taken place, the atmosphere has bordered on hysteria. You could say . . . well . . . it's like sitting on an atomic bomb waiting for it to go off. Before we get started, I always stand in front of the screen and photograph the students in the cinema auditorium, all keyed up and ready to go in their Christmas jumpers and Santa hats, their spoons and inflatable American footballs held aloft (see fig. 8.1).

As the years go on, I'm finding that more and more students have seen both *The Room* and James Franco's *The Disaster Artist* and have read Sestero's tell-all story. They don't need to Google in advance. Some students have even been to the Prince Charles, as I have, so you'd think they would consider a screening with their lecturer to be the most achingly unhip thing or just bullshit teaching and they either wouldn't turn up or wouldn't participate. After all, Tommy is *kind of* a cautionary tale. He is so earnest and naive, so outrageous and immersed in his performance. He is, well . . . kind of mortifying. Nope. They love it. From the first "Hey, Denny!" to the manic/sarcastic/relieved applause that rings around the auditorium as the end credits roll, the students really immerse themselves and take all manner of creative chances. They might initially rely on the cheat sheet and follow my lead (I always sit in the

8.1 De Montfort University students at a screening of *The Room*. Courtesy of Ellen Wright.

front row so they can see me getting involved and hopefully feel less inhibited with their own callouts), but gradually they begin to improvise and become more raucous all on their own. It's always great to hear the stifled giggles and sneakily turn to see a sea of illuminated mobile phone screens swaying in unison throughout the first mortifying sex scene, to hear the first rallying cry of "*Spoon*!" and, out of the corner of my eye, see one whiz past me, followed by several more. I feel absurdly proud. It's like the very best kind of cabaret, but I don't *really* see it, more I hear and *feel* it.

When students come to university they are at a pivotal stage in their lives. They are often still finding their feet as people. Like so many young adults, they are worried about embarrassing themselves, about taking a chance, playing and performing and being perceived as foolish or childish. *The Room* offers a release valve from all these pressures. Their exuberant participation and reactions seem to bear this out.

Every year in my module feedback, students beg to be taken on a trip to the Prince Charles Cinema for another fix. Unfortunately, it's not doable. However, over the years, after they have finished their degrees, some have contacted me on social media to show me pictures of themselves at the Prince Charles, ready for round two. Elsewhere in their module feedback, they tell me how much they enjoy the module, and, even more hearteningly, they get *really* good marks. In their end-of-term papers, lots of the students write on *The Room* or on cult spaces as permissive spaces.

That's not all. Students' assessed assignments have examined deeper issues, such as sexism in *The Room* and the fact that, just as Dyer observes, what is utopia for some may not be a utopia for all, with some cult screening spaces being or having been problematic for ethnic minority, female, and LGBT+ audiences; the problematic way in which *The Room* portrays white, heterosexual, American masculinity; and the ways in which ironic appreciation of the film can liberate and empower audiences. I have also read works explaining how, despite cult film screenings often being understood to have an anything-goes policy, there are actually unwritten rules to being part of a cult film audience; how Tommy is a hero or god and fans of *The Room* are his worshippers, with a very distinct set of rituals through which they express their admiration; and how "playing up" can be a means for *The Room*'s fans to seek acceptance from fellow fans.

Other works have drawn on fields as diverse as psychology, social history, and philosophy to demonstrate the creativity, skill, awareness, and diversity of *The Room*'s fans and the richness of *The Room* as a cultural encounter. I really do think that the interactive screening of *The Room* plays a big part in the students really understanding just what is so special about cult film and the cult film experience more broadly.

ELLEN WRIGHT is Senior Lecturer in Cinema and Television History at De Montfort University. Her work appears in *Celebrity Studies*.

Notes

1. See McCulloch, "'Most People Bring Their Own Spoons,'" 189–218.
2. Mathijs and Sexton, *Cult Cinema*, 19.
3. Dyer, *Only Entertainment*, 20.

9 THE ROOM IN THE CLASSROOM

HOW I USE A BAD MOVIE TO TEACH GOOD FILMMAKING

ROSS MORIN

I feel like I'm sitting on an atomic bomb waiting for it to go off!

—Steven, *The Room*

Film schools commonly teach film production by studying classic works like *Citizen Kane.* That is, they dissect films that are masterfully executed in almost every way. I teach film production by studying *The Room,* but for the opposite reason: in almost every way, it is so masterfully *inept. The Room* is as bad as *Citizen Kane* is good, and that makes it just as valuable. When I described *The Room* to *Entertainment Weekly* as "the *Citizen Kane* of bad movies," I meant it could tell us just as much about the fundamentals of cinematic craft—maybe even more.

There is something magical about *The Room.* The film awakens a sense of wonder, shock, and embarrassment in all who see it. I find that my students are often bored with and disconnected from "stuffy" films that have been secured in the academic canon for decades, like *Citizen Kane,* but *The Room,* a film that runs counter to everything that the canon represents, activates them immediately. Even while watching the film for fun, students are engaged in intellectual deconstruction as they provide humorous critical commentary and heckle the film. As a teaching tool, *The Room* serves as a sort of Trojan horse—assignments begin by eliciting laughter from students and seamlessly transition to rigorous analysis. *The Room* allows me to harness their joy and passion for bad cinema to motivate them to learn what makes cinema "good."

In this chapter, I'll share examples of how I integrate *The Room* into my undergraduate filmmaking courses and argue that bad films—*The Room* in particular—are just as effective as good ones when it comes to teaching. My pedagogical philosophy is that it is as important to teach what *not* to do as it is to teach what *to* do. For the former purpose, there is no better resource than *The Room*.

Dismantling an Atomic Bomb

In my screenwriting class, after I teach the foundations of drama, I assign each student a scene from *The Room* and three tasks. The first calls for students to watch their scene and transcribe the dialogue and action word for word. The very process of transcription yields vivid, affective moments of discovery. They can *feel* the script literally wasting their time as they type. Every "Oh hi" becomes a personal offense, every "ha ha" a stolen moment of life they can never get back. As they transcribe, they *endure* the lack of conflict, the interminable paragraphs of dialogue, and the redundancy of actions; consciously or not, they are engaged in the process of identifying elements of bad writing. (For a longer discussion of waste in *The Room*, see chapter 13.)

The second task advances beyond identification to analysis of fundamentals of dramatic structure, such as character objectives, conflict, rising action, climax, and resolution. Since most scenes in the film lack *all* of these elements yet are full of dialogue, students observe that writing good drama is more than just putting words on a page. Students learn to articulate why exposition ("We got a new client at the bank; we make a lot of money."); characters ("You remember my friend Shirley Hamilton?"); and action ("OK, let's go to the couch, and we will sit down.") need a coherent cause and effect that progresses the plot, develops inner psychology, and raises the stakes.

The third task asks students to distill and shorten their transcriptions to their essential elements by deleting any dialogue or actions that are irrelevant to the drama. For example, a student tasked with transcribing the opening five-page sequence may reduce it to a half page in which the only drama is whether Denny will be invited to watch Johnny and Lisa have sex. When the drama is laid bare, without the noise of meaningless dialogue, the distillation serves as an x-ray of the scene, revealing how the dramatic structure fails—or, in most cases, how there was no drama in the scene at all.

After this assignment, students look at their own screenplays and wonder, "Am *I* writing like Wiseau?" They see their story problems more clearly and inquire, "What *is* supposed to be in a scene?" and are even more motivated to study how successful screenplays are written.

In my directing class, I assign the script for the scene where Mark almost throws Peter off the roof. It is mostly a conventional three-act structure, yet it still contains the film's characteristic absurdity, such as the marijuana that makes Mark both suicidal *and* homicidal. The first part of the assignment is to analyze the subtext of the dialogue solely on the basis of the script and then compare it to the performances in the film. When studying lines like "Why do you want to know my secret, man? Well, you're right! It's Lisa. I don't know what to do, man. I'm so depressed," students discover that Wiseau directed the scene as if there were no subtext in the line delivery—each character means exactly what they say.

In the second part of the assignment, students are challenged to construct meaningful drama out of the script as they direct it word for word with their own actors. Students dig into character psychology to create subtext and dramatic beats that do not exist literally on the page.

For example, Peter's line "What are you, nuts?" evolves from a straightforward question about Mark's sanity to a threat, a plea for safety, or even an appeal to Mark's unconditional love.

Students become psychological detectives solving a dramatic mystery, finding meaning in the incoherence. They learn that dialogue rarely means what it looks like, and as writers and directors, they think in deeper ways about their own screenplays.

I teach blocking (the spatial positioning of actors in relation to one another and to the camera) using the scene where Denny, Mark, and Peter enter dressed in tuxedos (see fig. 9.1). As the scene starts, Johnny stands awkwardly frozen by a table and speaks with Denny, who stands robotically still with a football. Denny then gracefully pivots and moves out of the way *before* the doorbell rings. Peter enters, sits in a chair facing the camera—not the other characters—and adjusts his cuffs. Denny opens the door a second time to reveal a clean-shaven Mark, and the camera dollies in to a close-up. In attempts to make "sense" of the blocking choices, inevitably a number of burning questions present themselves: Why is Peter facing away from everyone? Why is Tommy standing near the table? Why is Denny between Mark and Johnny? Students laugh as they fail to come up with answers, and they recognize the importance of motivated blocking decisions. Finally, we study examples of successful cinematic blocking, and I teach them to draw blocking diagrams for their own films and require that they articulate the dramatic purpose of each of their choices.

In my cinematography class, we begin by identifying the funny and weird mistakes in the film, like soft-focus shots, lack of window gels, and framing that cuts off heads, and then move on to analyzing light sources and motivation. In the daytime living room scenes, every window from every wall seems to cast shadows equally, as if there are four different suns outside. Students analyze each light source on the

9.1. Mark, Denny, Peter, and Tommy in tuxes. © 2003 by Wiseau-Films. (Movie still from *The Room*.)

basis of brightness, color, shadow softness, and direction, and once they do, they realize they're looking at an enigmatic, M. C. Escher–esque lighting scenario. Students then reverse engineer the lighting setup via an overhead diagram, hypothesizing how the cinematographer lit the scene. Finally, they present how they would solve the lighting issues if they were hired to reshoot the scenes.

When I teach montage in my editing class, I screen classic examples like the Odessa Steps scene from *Battleship Potemkin*, the training sequence from *Rocky*, the falling out of love from *Citizen Kane*, and, of course, the first sex scene from *The Room*. In the former cases, I teach the fundamentals of "good" editing—from graphic connections and collisions to tempo and rhythm. When we get to *The Room*, I pose unanswerable questions: Why put those two shots in succession? Why cut at *that* particular frame? Why show Johnny's abs *again*? Through these questions, I get students to think about the meaning (or lack thereof) behind editing choices.

The Room reflects amateur editing instincts. When asked to create a montage, students often think only about the *content* of shots and the music but not about the actual editing technique that goes into it. One can imagine Wiseau thinking similarly: "Shots of lovemaking, roses, and candles. Music about love. And five minutes long." When studying editing in *The Room*, students discover that editing is more than just cutting a series of shots together, and they are energized to learn the craft in the process.

There are two sound elements I teach with *The Room*. The first is automated dialogue replacement (ADR; dialogue recorded and edited in postproduction). I skip over my remarks on performance ("Anything for my princess!"), focusing instead just on recording technique. I screen the scene where Lisa first seduces Mark and ask students to identify why it sounds so odd. They usually remark that the dialogue sounds too "present," like a National Public Radio interview, and they want to know why. I then teach the differences between lavalier and shotgun microphones, or between dynamic, condenser, and ribbon microphones, and follow up with discussions about proper placement for each. Students respond by suggesting ways they would have recorded the ADR differently, such as using shotgun or condenser microphones placed at more of a distance from the actors during the recording process to simulate how the dialogue would have actually been recorded on set.

The second element of sound I teach is Foley (the recording of sound effects after shooting). In the same seduction scene, Lisa pours red wine off-screen. Before she brings the glass into frame, I pause and ask students how much wine they think is in the glass given what they heard. Students usually guess nearly half the bottle. However, when she reveals the glass, it's only a small pour, which elicits students' laughter and confusion. Staying on the topic of glass-related Foley, I also screen the scene where Johnny drunkenly drops his whiskey glass and it breaks off-screen. I ask students what they think happened on the basis of the Foley, and they guess that the glass *exploded* as if thrown against a brick wall. In both examples, I ask students to analyze why they are laughing, and they reply that it's because the sound is so incongruous with what actually happens. These examples teach the importance of sound in constructing off-screen space in the mind of the audience.

The Guerrero Street Paradox

In weekly presentations in my screenwriting class, students address representational issues in *The Room*, with particular attention to sex and gender. After only a few weeks of analyzing the film, they identify clear patterns of misogyny and discuss how the film is unrelenting in its vilification and sexualization of women. They remark on its casual discussion of domestic abuse: "I used to know a girl, she had a dozen guys. One of them found out about it, beat her up so bad she ended up in a hospital on Guerrero Street." (The rejoinder to this disturbing anecdote: "Ha ha, what a story, Mark!") Students highlight the representation of Lisa ("Such a manipulative bitch!"; "tramp"; "devil"), as well as the film's attitudes toward women in general ("Sometimes they're just too smart, sometimes they're just flat-out stupid, other times they're just evil"). Students analyze actions and behavior that show women with no purpose other than to shop, day drink, and please men sexually. Students articulate how *The Room*, scene after scene, represents women as weak, yet evil, tricksters who need to be controlled by men.

At first, students are amused. They hypothesize that writer-director Wiseau had his heart broken and that the film is his attempt to vindicate himself as a good man (for only an *evil* woman would have left him). "I treat you like a princess, and you stab me in the back. . . . How could you love him!?" Johnny despairs in yet another unforgettable scene. His expressions of pain are so Old Testament baroque that they're laughable.

But after weeks of laughing at the film's sexism, they tend to shift from amused to concerned. Students question whether it is morally permissible to laugh at the misogyny of *The Room*. Beyond laughter, they question what it means when audiences participate in the viewing by yelling lines such as "Get out of my life, you bitch!" along with Johnny and Mark. Their apprehension leads to discussions of the politics of camp and audience participation and appropriation of a text. They often say they're being ironic, or even subversive of the film's politics, by performing "sexism" with a wink. When I hear this, I push back against the assertions. I ask, "Are you laughing *at* the film, or *with* the film? How subversive is it to yell obscenities at a woman on-screen?" The discussion then shifts from sexism *within* the film to sexism in *watching* the film, as we explore some of the larger philosophical and political questions of feminist film theory.

Obviously, the problem of representation of women extends far beyond *The Room*, and that is why the film is such a valuable teaching tool: when students learn to identify and analyze the bigoted representations in *The Room*, they start to see similar patterns in mainstream TV and film. Alongside our dissection of *The Room*, I show examples from Marvel films or *The Fast and the Furious* series, and we explore how the same misogyny is present—it's just hidden with better expertise. One of the main lessons for students is that the analysis of craft and the analysis of representational ethics not only go hand in hand but are essentially inextricable. *The Room* isn't remarkable because the film is so misogynistic (Hollywood is already there); it's remarkable because the failures of craft make the misogyny so visible.

Sometimes film students think that film production classes should be separate from film theory. After these discussions, however, many of my students say they are determined to never make a film with politics like those of *The Room*. Wiseau is a perfect example of what can happen when someone with no background in film theory is given free rein to make a film. Because of him, most of my students grow committed to the integration of film practice and theory, with emphasis on their own social and ethical responsibility as filmmakers.

Seeing Ourselves in *The Room*

In an interview included as a special feature on the 2005 DVD release of the movie, Wiseau argues that "*The Room* teaches us what not to do." I couldn't agree more. Bad movies like *The Room* illustrate filmmaking mistakes and problems, and good movies like *Citizen Kane* highlight innovations and solutions. It's equally important for students to see bad cinema as something to work *away from* as it is to see good cinema as something to work *toward*.

I think that young filmmakers connect to *The Room* because they can see themselves and their own instincts reflected back to them. They aren't *that* far away from making something so terrible. They, too, are striving for greatness and . . . well . . . they are not quite there yet. It can be difficult for students to identify with Oscar-winning films by renowned filmmakers who have seemingly endless talent and budgets, but *The Room* is relatable; they could make it themselves, today. While films like *Citizen Kane* give students something to aspire to in the future, *The Room* helps them think about the work they're making *right now*.

There are so many ways to fail at making a film. *The Room* makes it OK to fail and to talk about failure. Students often feel disheartened when they realize how much more they need to learn to make a good film. When students study and laugh at *The Room* as a classroom community, they are also laughing at the shortcomings of their own films, and that can bring a sense of fellowship and comfort with one another. The same humor that unites students in their love of watching and heckling *The Room* unites them as fledgling filmmakers making their first missteps together. When I bring *The Room* into the classroom, I'm harnessing humor to help students see and accept their mistakes, and then I teach them the skills to improve and grow. *The Room* is the most impactful way I teach filmmaking, and for that, I am thankful to Tommy Wiseau. *The Room* has made my students better filmmakers and me a better teacher.

Acknowledgments

Thanks to Evan Clar, Clark Collis, Greg Sestero, Lindsay Crawford, Simon Feldman, and Stuart Vyse—and to my students for providing so many of the insights I highlighted in this piece.

ROSS MORIN is Associate Professor of Film Studies at Connecticut College. He is an independent filmmaker, editor, and cinematographer.

FOR THE LOVE OF CULT; 10

OR, HOW I LEARNED TO STOP WORRYING AND BUILD MY OWN SCREENING OF *THE ROOM*

AMANDA ANN KLEIN

In the fall of 2009, under the guise of teaching a preexisting class on film aesthetics, I designed a brand-new course for the purpose of screening *The Room*, Trash Cinema and Taste. Though most film studies courses strive to provide students with the accepted canon of "quality films" like *Casablanca, Citizen Kane,* and *Vertigo,* this course focused on texts that were notorious, not for their excellence but for their terribleness. The course would examine American films that have been marginalized because of a variety of interrelated factors: their small budgets and chintzy set designs (*Sins of the Fleshapoids*); their completely inept style (*Glen or Glenda*); their offensive subject matter (*Pink Flamingos* and *Superstar: The Karen Carpenter Story*); their violent or sexual imagery (*Two Thousand Maniacs!* and *Bad Girls Go to Hell*); and their desire to place marginalized faces at the center of the screen (*Freaks* and *Blacula*). My students and I discussed why these films have historically been viewed as "trash," relying heavily on Pierre Bourdieu's useful one-liner, "Taste classifies and classifies the classifier,"[1] to answer this question. Students learn how and why classifying popular culture as being in "good" or "bad" taste tells us a lot about how unnatural and constructed such categories can be.

The polished Hollywood stalwarts that populate the syllabi of many film studies courses are so seamlessly crafted and carry the weight of so much critical praise that it is often difficult for novice (and seasoned) film students to find a way to analyze their "invisible" style. As film scholar Jeffrey Sconce argues, "beach blanket films, Elvis pictures, 1950s monster-movies—any film where history and technique remove students from the 'effects' of representation and plunge them headlong into the quagmire of signification itself" can become fruitful classroom texts.[2] Students have grown up consuming the language of cinema—they are its native speakers—and so they often fail to recognize what they already know, as they rarely watch films that lack the "effects of representation."

A film like *The Room*, however, violates almost every rule of storytelling: characters pop in and out of scenes with little explanation, plotlines are addressed and then dropped forever (Lisa's mother's cancer, Denny's drug problems, etc.), and character dialogue is frequently nonsensical ("Leave your stupid comments in your pocket!"). The film also "mistranslates" most editing conventions by inserting multiple establishing shots of San Francisco into the middle of a single party scene and lacks any form of spatial continuity (does Johnny live in an apartment or a house, and how does everyone get up to that roof deck anyway?). In these moments, all the seams of the film, the mismatched and poorly executed fabrics of its construction, are visible. Whatever story *The Room* means to tell is completely overshadowed by its nearly infinite mishaps. It proposes itself to be taken extremely seriously, and yet we cannot take the film seriously because it is so over the top. Wiseau's unadulterated passion and hubris render his errors all the more engaging—and conspicuous. The politics of taste and the man behind the curtain are easily overlooked when we only see Ingrid Bergman framed in a beautifully lit close-up, nuzzling under Humphrey Bogart's reassuring jawline.

As much fun as it was to watch and discuss these films with my students, we all knew what the class was really for: to put on Greenville,

10.1 Still from a video mash-up transforming characters from *The Room* into the intro of *Friends*. Courtesy of Ross John Fearnley/ The Unusual Suspect.

North Carolina's first ever public screening of *The Room*. I knew it was unlikely that I would ever find a theater in town screening the movie. At the time, Greenville's local multiplexes mainly carried mainstream Hollywood releases, with independent or foreign films only appearing after the announcement of Academy Award nominations, when local theaters looked to capitalize on Oscar excitement. And where I lived, there were no repertory movie theaters or university-sponsored film series, two venues where a non-first-run film might be played.

In fact, when I first saw Tommy Wiseau's opus, I watched it alone, in my den. I would not advise doing this, as its greatness is best enjoyed with a raucous, spoon-throwing crowd. When my solitary screening concluded, just moments after a distraught Johnny commits suicide with Chekhov's recently discovered handgun, I had an epiphany: if I wanted to experience *The Room* properly—that is, in a theater packed with rowdy, spoon-tossing cynics—I would have to create the screening myself. And that's exactly what I did.

There was an additional wrinkle, though. This assignment wasn't just about watching a movie—it was about participating in the cult experience from start to finish. Students' grades for this class project would be partially determined by the number of people in the audience and the level of enthusiasm emanating from them during the screening. Just as classic exploitation filmmakers like Kroger Babb and David Friedman endeavored to fill as many theater seats as possible because their livelihoods depended on it, my students had to fill the theater as if their grades depended on it—because they did. I directed students to say or do whatever they needed to do to fill the seats.

I encouraged them to think of their advertising the way Babb and Friedman once did, as "ballyhoo"—as an exaggeration or complete misrepresentation of the experience of attending *The Room*. Media historian Eric Schaefer defines ballyhoo as "that noisy, vulgar spiel that drew audiences to circuses and sideshows . . . a hyperbolic excess of words and images that sparked the imagination."[3] Ballyhoo promises audiences something—a controversial image, a novel experience, or a visceral reaction ("so scary you'll die of fright!")—that it does not fulfill. This unfulfilled promise is a convention of exploitation advertising. The students were given the duration of the semester to design an ad campaign, distribute posters and flyers, create a buzz in various forms of media, and prepare the venue for the night of the screening—just as Kroger Babb once did while promoting classic exploitation fare like *Mom and Dad*. One might reasonably argue that Wiseau engaged in plenty of ballyhoo himself, albeit unintentionally, with one of *The Room*'s original promos famously declaring the movie had "the passion of Tennese [*sic*] Williams."

When I first offered this class, in 2009, my students were at a big disadvantage compared to those who took it in a post–*Disaster Artist* world. Back then, very few East Carolina University students had heard of *The Room*, which meant my students had to convince a fickle pack of young adults to give up a night of drinking to sit through a "bad" movie they had never heard of before. Indeed, the main objective of the project was to teach students about how cult film audiences are created and nurtured. This was the trickiest aspect of the class assignment because a cult audience is, by definition, spontaneous in nature. Some scholars define cult films by their aesthetics, their budgets, their critical reception, or their production histories. But at the end of the day, a cult film is only as good as the audience who is there, at that moment. A cult is created *by* the audience, not by a group of students hoping to score an A in the film studies class they're taking to fulfill a college graduation requirement. How would they get their peers to attend? How would they convey the value of this viewing experience? Could a group of students (the majority of whom had never seen *The Room* prior to enrolling in my course) *create* a cult film audience out of sheer force of will?

By the night of the screening, I think my students were legitimate *The Room* enthusiasts, but what of the audience members who had been lured into the theater on a weeknight, because the advertising falsely promised the screening event of a lifetime, or because their friends in the class had begged them to, or because they were promised special prizes? It was the students' responsibility to prepare the audience for the evening's events through their promotional efforts and also through their presentation of a brief introduction to the film. Such introductions had been perfected by exploiteers, who, ostensibly motivated by the desire to "educate" their bewildered audience, would often bring in "experts" (or actors dressed as doctors and nurses) to speak to those who came to watch their exploitation films about venereal disease and "white slavery." But, of course, this was titillation in the guise of education, which further added to the experience of watching the film. Students attempted to replicate this environment by enlisting one of their classmates to serve as an emcee. She provided the audience with insight into the cult of *The Room*, demonstrated some of its key rituals (such as yelling "Hi, Denny!" every time the character appeared on-screen), and interacted with the audience throughout her introduction, which prepped them for the film to come. This is key to a successful cult film screening: making sure everyone in the audience is on the same page. By the time the credits roll, the screening should feel like a collaborative effort.

The students were also tasked with assembling prop bags for the audience and deciding which rituals they wanted the audience to perform. They repeated some of the most basic rites of viewing *The Room*—the throwing of spoons, the shouting of "Because you're a woman!" every time Lisa offered up an excuse for her duplicitous behavior, and the tossing of footballs whenever Johnny plays football on-screen (which is, weirdly, a lot)[4]—but they also added a few new ones. First, during each of the film's lengthy and grotesque lovemaking scenes, students wandered through the audience with bunches of fake red roses (because Johnny and Lisa make love on a pile of roses, twice). They would tap an audience member on the shoulder and whisper, "Welcome to the sex scene. Please accept this rose." It's already uncomfortable watching Johnny make love to Lisa's belly button, but to have someone offer you a rose during such an awkward scene is truly unnerving. The second ritual they added was to release several garbage bags' worth of balloons during the film's climactic (and lengthy) party scene. Once the balloons were released, the audience began to bat them around (they would pop after hitting the ceiling), thus bringing the on-screen party into the theater.

When the event was over, I asked students to submit a paper describing what they had learned from participating in this screening project. Many students wrote that it had allowed them to experience firsthand what we had been reading about and discussing all semester: the intimate relationship between cult films and their audiences and the ways cult films attract and maintain committed fans.

Since that first screening, I have continued to teach my course on trash cinema five more times, which means I have been able to attend exactly five interactive screenings of *The Room*, organized by five very different cohorts of college students. Each year the event comes out a little differently. What I like best is the way this project builds a sense of community and camaraderie among the students. The night of the event, there is always an excitement that comes with putting on a show. I think students learned—firsthand—what it would be like to be an exploiteer, someone whose livelihood depended on generating enough ballyhoo to fill a theater. They also learned about the joys and rewards of cult viewership (even if the viewership they created was highly constructed and mediated through the lens of a class project). But mostly? I'm delighted that the students learned about the joy of creating a shared taste culture, a community that's all-in on the same joke. At a time when we're no longer reading the same newspapers (and most newspapers are gone anyway), or even believing in the same set of facts (like whether or not a hurricane will hit Alabama), it's comforting to share a communal experience, to come together, for the love of what is truly bad.

AMANDA ANN KLEIN is Associate Professor of Film Studies at East Carolina University. She is author of *Millennials Killed the Video Star: MTV's Transition to Reality Programming* and of *American Film*

Cycles: Reframing Genres, Screening Social Problems, and Defining Subcultures. She is editor (with R. Barton Palmer) of *Cycles, Sequels, Spin-offs, Remakes, and Reboots: Multiplicities in Film and Television*.

Notes

1. Bourdieu, *Distinction*.
2. Sconce, "Esper, the Renunciator," 31.
3. Schaefer, "*Bold! Daring! Shocking! True!*," 103.
4. See Collis, "Crazy Cult of *The Room*."

PART IV
FAN RECEPTION

HOW CAN THEY SAY THIS ABOUT ME? 11

RIFFING JOHNNY, LISA, AND DENNY IN ONLINE HOME-BREW COMMENTARIES OF THE ROOM

MATT FOY

Sitting down with *The Room* for the first time (or first dozen times) leaves myriad things unclear and many questions unanswered. Fans seeking explanations, however, will not find them on official Blu-ray and DVD copies of *The Room,* for as often as director and star Tommy Wiseau has discussed his magnum opus in interview format, he has never produced a feature-length commentary track.

In that absence, everyday film critics and movie "riffers" have spawned a small cottage industry of their own internet-circulated home-brew commentaries. A combination of underground cultural cachet and obvious aesthetic and narrative flaws makes *The Room* an accessible target for scathing running commentary. A simple web search reveals a wealth of internet-based commentaries on *The Room,* ranging from carefully scripted verbal dissections by internet-famous acts to stream-of-consciousness commentaries posted to YouTube with a few dozen views.

In each one, commenters riff, or critically talk back to, the film by identifying a symbol embedded in the text—a line of dialogue, a character's behavior, a subtextual element—while the symbol is on the screen, drawing attention to the ways the film encodes messages through dialogue, symbolism, tropes, and iconography. The process grants the riffer the opportunity to rhetorically deconstruct the meanings foregrounded in the text with acts of micro-criticism rather than making sense of it in retrospect, as in a review. Circulated over the internet and circumventing copyright laws and YouTube digital rights management takedowns, such commentaries serve as an important and influential supplement to *The Rocky Horror Picture Show*–esque mayhem of *The Room*'s iconic in-theater performance rituals.

We know online comedians and critics are talking about *The Room*, but what are they saying? This chapter samples discursive tactics used by critics and comedians in online commentaries of *The Room* and explores how they can be understood as meaningful responses to the messages embedded in the film. To be clear, the majority of commentary tracks available aim not at in-depth film criticism but to generate affirmative feedback from "audience members" (that is, viewers) in the form of likes, subscriptions, and positive comments. But even comedic or scornful criticisms have the potential to influence audiences' perceptions of not only the film at hand but a constellation of related ideas. Even a rhetorically crude comment such as "This movie sucks," when uttered before an engaged audience, communicates the utterer's attitude toward the film (or any mediated) text and calls on the audience to attach the stigma of "suck" to it. Thus, even dismissive or vulgar responses contain ideological implications from which critical meaning can be spun. As critic and scholar Kenneth Burke observed in his book *The Philosophy of Literary Form*, "An attitude may be reasonable or unreasonable; it may contain an adequate meaning or an inadequate meaning—but in either case, it would contain a meaning."[1]

For this chapter, I sampled online commentary tracks critiquing *The Room* available on YouTube or SoundCloud or for purchase on the authors' respective websites. I included only commentaries intended to be synced with and listened to concurrently with the film; reviews that discussed the film as a past object were not considered. Available commentaries surveyed included RiffTrax (the original 2014 riff and an updated 2016 version modeled after their live riffing of *The Room*), Collider Videos, the Disorderly, Geekverse, Jaboody Studios, Red Big'un, Red Letter Media, Reel Talk (Gonzalez), Real Politik, World Class Bullshitters, and 0816EGG Productions.[2] During my review, I noted recurring themes commenters employed to mock or criticize *The Room* and its performers, noting strategies used to reframe the characters and plot, among other things.

Fans of the cult television show *Mystery Science Theater 3000* (*MST3K*) will immediately recognize the tone and techniques commenters use to verbally dissect *The Room*. First airing in 1988 on KTMA TV, a local station in the Minneapolis–Saint Paul region, *MST3K* featured a man and two wisecracking robots mocking "cheesy movies" in space. The award-winning series "raised talking back to the TV into an art form," in the words of former *Time* magazine (and current *New York Times*) television critic James Poniewozik.[3] Along the way, it brought the comedic art of riffing cheesy movies into the cultural lexicon, and it's clear that a generation of sharp-tongued amateur critics were paying attention.

Solidly operating with post-*MST3K* affectation, commenters riffing *The Room* were universally antagonistic toward the film and its performers, and they use many of the same comedic strategies popularized by *MST3K*: making light of the film's many textual flaws, ridiculing its protagonists, interjecting unflattering intertextual references, placing incongruent dialogue in characters' mouths, and asserting alternate interpretations of the action unfolding on-screen. Commenters focused their criticisms on three characters: Johnny (and, by extension, Wiseau), Lisa, and Denny. Though *The Room* presents the trio as an ideal though nontraditional family unit (Johnny the patriarch, Lisa the matriarch, Denny the adopted child redeemed by Johnny) spoiled by Lisa's betrayal of Johnny, commenters engage in antagonistic counter-reading to (1) dispute the film's characterization of Johnny as an ideal patriarch, (2) dampen the film's insistence on Lisa's physical beauty while sympathizing with her relational woes, and (3) reimagine Denny from a product of Johnny's excellence to a disturbing, malevolent deviant. Using these tropes, commenters craft a humorous interpretation of the film that runs counter to the meanings presumably intended by Wiseau and the film's producers.

"He's Like a Mix between Jar Jar Binks, Frosty the Snowman, and PewDiePie"

The Room's hypervisible auteur receives the bulk of commenters' scorn, with multiple riffing tactics opposing the film's presentation of Johnny as a beacon of nurturing masculine heroism. Efforts to reduce and reframe Johnny begin with ridiculing his physical appearance. Johnny is variously described as "a catfish in a suit" and "a human piece of seasoned beef jerky" (RiffTrax), "wrinkly and lumpy—like a burn victim" (Jaboody), and a man who resembles "Jeff Goldblum mid-*Fly* transformation" (the Disorderly). His fashion sense is mocked—"He never has his tie fixed" (Reel Talk); "Why is he wearing a suit that's tailored for Andre the Giant?" (Red Letter Media)—as are his bodily movements, as commenters suggest he takes "little baby steps like something's up his ass" (Jaboody) and "walks like he has to take a morning shit" (World Class Bullshitters).

Commenters play Johnny's trademark "Oh hi" greeting to the hilt to reframe Johnny as deranged rather than jovial. They also imagine Johnny greeting inanimate objects: "Oh hi, garage" (0816EGG); "Oh hi, lamp" (Red Big'un). The RiffTrax crew relies heavily on the "Oh hi" trope to establish Johnny as unmoored from reality. In the voice of Johnny, RiffTrax performer Bill Corbett says, "Oh hi, Jeffy from the

11.1 A 2016 RiffTrax Live! screening of *The Room*. © 2016 by RiffTrax. Courtesy of Erik Peterson/RiffTrax.

Family Circus," when Johnny picks up a newspaper. When Johnny attempts to expose Lisa's infidelity by playing the recordings he has made of Lisa and Mark's conversations, Kevin Murphy (as Johnny) greets Mark's recorded voice with "Oh, hi Mark," before Corbett reminds Johnny that Mark isn't really there. Corbett defuses Johnny's climactic suicide by having him greet the gun he puts in his mouth: "Oh hi, gun barrel."

Commenters work to otherize Wiseau, who in interviews identifies as American, by insisting he is ambiguously foreign. When Lisa pours Mark a glass of wine, RiffTrax states: "This is a selection from Tommy Wiseau Vineyards. Nobody knows what country it comes from and most people don't want it at the table while they're eating." 0816EGG introduces a trope in which Wiseau's homeland is "Greekland": "the world's biggest exporter of giant metal storage crates . . . and pictures of spoons." In conjuring a backstory for Wiseau that explains his capacity to self-fund his $6 million film (as the figure has been widely reported), Reel Politik imagines him as "an oligarch who became rich overnight when the Berlin Wall fell" and "owned half the fucking hospitals in Poland."

As so often happens in discussions of *The Room,* commenters tend to treat Johnny the character and Wiseau the person as one, suggesting that Johnny's immaculate character is Wiseau projecting his own self-image onto the screen. "I feel like the people around Johnny make him look like he's a better person," Geekverse explains. "Johnny the actual person is nice—he does nice things—but he's a piece-of-shit kind of person. The way he talks about women is quite crude." "Some girl clearly broke his heart," the Disorderly suggests, "and this is kind of a revenge fantasy." Here, we glimpse the push-pull dynamic of commenters' counter-reading of the film. Pushed to adore Johnny in every way, from his muscular body to his material generosity to his wisdom when it comes to solving friends' problems, commenters respond by gleefully tearing down the perfect idol of himself Wiseau has constructed. "You kind of feel bad for Johnny in the end," Reel Talk muses in regard to Johnny's betrayal and suicide before reminding themselves, and the audience, "No, you don't."

"You Make Helen of Troy Look like a Pile of Shit"

Anyone who has experienced *The Room*'s in-theater audience rituals will be familiar with their hostility toward Lisa. In addition to the recurring "because you're a woman!" motif, Lisa is regularly criticized for her figure and cursed for her promiscuity. Within the film's projected worldview, hatred toward Lisa is the expected response: Johnny, the film insists, treats her immaculately; her betrayal of his affection and generosity is thus evil. Online riffers tend to conform with the film's misogyny, participating in what cultural studies theorist Stuart Hall termed *dominant-hegemonic* reading: accepting the dominant codes bestowed on the text by producers and reading the hegemonic message accordingly.[4]

Commenters ridicule Lisa's body and appearance often, reminding us that mocking a film is not the same as contradicting it. "I know this is going to sound horrible, but she's kind of like Miss Piggy," Jaboody opines, beginning a mini-trope of speaking as Lisa with a Miss Piggy inflection ("Oh Denny Boy"; "Mind Your Own Business, *Mom*"). "I can't stand Lisa's buck teeth," Reel Talk states. "It looks like her tongue is in jail." Several commenters endorsed the film's hatred for Lisa because of her unfaithfulness to Johnny and her pursuit of Mark. Reel Talk explains, "She's probably one of the biggest sluts in film history; she's not a slut because she's having sex, it's because she's having sex with his best friend."

At times, commenters offer an explicit motivation for cursing Lisa: countering the film's problematically misogynistic construction of women. They accept the film's premise that Lisa is a "duplicitous harpy," in Reel Politik's language, but pass the blame to the film's scribe, Wiseau. In attacking Lisa, commenters communicated disdain for Wiseau, criticizing him for failing to understand women and attributing to him a misogynistic autobiographical revenge fantasy. "You watch this movie: it feels like it was thought up by someone who's never talked to a woman before," Red Letter Media suggests. "If you look at this movie as a passion project written by this man, it's incredibly sexist. . . . But it's almost like he's too innocent to get mad at. We're like, he doesn't know any better." "*The Room* is kind of about an abusive relationship told from the perspective of someone who doesn't know they're abusive," Reel Politik observes. "He's been hurt. He's been through some heartbreak," Jaboody speculates. Impersonating Wiseau, Jaboody adds, "Bitch, this is you."

That commenters blame Wiseau even while ridiculing Lisa is evident in their handling of the film's notorious sex scenes. Though commenters mocked the sex scenes between Mark and Lisa—"The year this movie came out, 70 percent of homes with spiral staircases had them demolished" (RiffTrax)—they were demonstratively more hostile toward the scenes of Johnny and Lisa: "He's definitely fucking her belly button, and she is just trying her hardest not to puke" (the Disorderly). "The wormy thrusting, that's what really dares you not to run screaming into the night" (RiffTrax).

Though the film insists that the audience sympathize with Johnny because of Lisa's infidelity, commenters were quick to identify with Lisa. "If I were Lisa," World Class Bullshitters assert, "I'd pick Mark over Johnny. Johnny's a goon with a tiny dick." When Lisa and Mark have sex, Jaboody imagines her saying, "When Tommy's entering my belly button, I think of you. I want you to turn my outie into an innie." Both Reel Politik and Jaboody observe that while Johnny's naked body is prominently displayed during sex, Mark remains covered. "He's doing everything to not show his mate's hot bod . . . what a conceited man" (Reel Politik).

"Is This the Origin Story of the BTK [Killer]?"

Though Mark is the third member of *The Room*'s love triangle and Lisa's accomplice, he is comparatively spared from the worst of commenters' scorn, aside from some gentle riffing on his appearance and "creepy 80s rock guitarist beard" (Collider). For commenters, the other man defiling Johnny and Lisa's house is not Mark but Denny, Johnny and Lisa's peculiar neighbor, whose sexual confusion and ambiguous maturity make him a versatile cipher for imposing deviant motivations. Because even the movie can't answer what Denny "does"—when Claudette asks Lisa that question, Lisa launches into a speech about Johnny's benevolence—commenters gleefully fill that void with a wide range of sinister perversions.

Through riffing, Denny becomes a morass of unspeakable things. He is a stalker: "He looks like a fucking psychopath. . . . Denny makes me feel uncomfortable. He's always just there, lurking" (Geekverse). He is a perverted man-child: "Denny, he's imagined Pokémons having sex" (RiffTrax). He is a dangerous voyeur who's "going to be in the corner jerking off" (Jaboody) to Johnny and Lisa having sex. Ultimately, he is a necrophiliac: "Is he going to hump [Johnny's post-suicide] body like Johnny humped the dress just now?" (Red Big'un).

Because Denny is a far more ill-defined character than the hyper-defined Johnny (perfect good) and Lisa (perfect evil), commenters' verbal defiling of Denny functions less as a reframing of the character and more as a counterweight to the idyllic (if nontraditional) family unit that Wiseau has constructed for Johnny. Within the film's narrative, Denny exists merely to reaffirm Johnny's bottomless compassion and generosity, whether it comes to money, shelter, or wisdom; he is a commercial for what Johnny can do for those around him. At the film's conclusion, Denny is the audience's avatar, signaling that it is time to mourn Johnny while blaming Lisa and Mark (especially the former, for the latter repents and discards Lisa). Rather than following Denny's lead and paying tribute to Johnny, however, commenters seize one last chance to verbally defile both: "No, Denny, leave [dead Johnny's] pants on" (RiffTrax).

The three riffing themes discussed above do not constitute an exhaustive list of criticisms employed in online home-brew commentary tracks of *The Room*. No character or scene is spared. Commenters gleefully degrade the film by pointing out aesthetic shortcomings (Jaboody: "Dude, six-million-dollar budget and they couldn't shoot on a real fucking roof?") and continuity issues (0816EGG: "She put her glass down, then she put her hand away, then she put her glass down again in the next shot"). They distract from the film's plot by interjecting intertextual references (RiffTrax: "This week on *Full House*, the Tanners get a creepy new neighbor"). Such comments collectively work toward a similar goal as the identified three themes: to disrupt *The Room*'s plot and discourage identification with the characters in the manner asserted by the film's producers.

The kind of derisive humor displayed in the commentaries discussed here will not appeal to every audience member. For those seeking commentary tracks that enlighten, contextualize, or offer insight into the film, filmmaker, or the art of filmmaking, commenters gleefully ridiculing a protagonist's appearance, shaming his fiancée, and framing their pseudo-ward as a deviant sex offender may read as destructive or uncharitable. Some discourses upon which they riff (women's bodies and slut shaming, hostility toward nontraditional English speakers, domestic violence, and suicide) tap into serious real-world issues that in most contexts are forbidden from mockery.

Their riffing is more than just antagonism for its own sake, though; commenters' hostility toward Johnny, Lisa, Denny, and company should also be read through the lens of the film to which it responds. Because the film stridently presents Johnny as wise, compassionate, and desirable, commenters counter-frame him as incoherent, incomprehensible, and physically grotesque. Because the film assaults the audience with insistence that Lisa is transcendentally beautiful, commenters counterattack by degrading her appearance. Because Denny exists only as a monument to Johnny, commenters deface the idol, chipping away at Johnny's patriarchal perfection while casting a pall over Johnny's construction of the American dream. All this in sum works to destabilize the film's simplistic constructions of heroism, patriarchy, and gender relations. Whether this cumulative response is more desirable than the film to which it responds will always warrant interrogation.

As Kenneth Burke suggests in *Permanence and Change*, "the spontaneous speech of a people is loaded with judgments. It is intensely moral—its names for objects contain the emotional overtones which give us the cues as to how we should act towards these objects."[5] Though (generally) loosely constructed and only occasionally generous toward their subject matter, the judgments passed on these commentary tracks are anything but ambiguous toward how they want audiences to approach *The Room*: with eyebrows raised and daggers aimed in all directions.

MATT FOY is Associate Professor of Communication at Upper Iowa University. He is Chief Journal Editor of *Professional Wrestling Studies Journal*. His work appears in *Popular Culture Studies Journal, Ohio Communication Journal, Southern Communication Journal*, and *Proteus: A Journal of Ideas*.

Notes

1. Burke, Philosophy of Literary Form, 43.

2. The list of commentaries referenced follows: Jen Gonzalez, "Episode 35: Reel Commentary: The Room," Reel Talk, November 28, 2017, https://www.reeltalkinc.com/episode-35-reel-commentary-room/; Red Letter Media, "The Room: Commentary Track," December 10, 2017, MP3 audio, https://redlettermedia.bandcamp.com/track/the-room-commentary-track; "The Room (2014)," RiffTrax, [Link no longer active]; "The Room," RiffTrax, March 8, 2016, MP3 audio, https://www.rifftrax.com/the-room-2016; Geekverse Podcast, "The Room Commentary Track," YouTube, December 1, 2017, https://www.youtube.com/watch?v=63Z-RsSsGDo; Jaboody Studios, "The Room Commentary Track," YouTube, June 25, 2016, https://www.youtube.com/watch?v=r4ACc8rxGn8; Red Big'un, "The Room Commentary," YouTube, May 1, 2018, https://www.youtube.com/watch?v=jfbOuKYCVes; World Class Bullshitters, "The Room Drunk Commentary Podcast: 500 Subscriber Special!," YouTube, June 11, 2016, https://www.youtube.com/watch?v=WgZB6mXQ2Po; Disorderly, "The Room DVD Commentary: Watch before You See The Disaster Artist," YouTube, December 4, 2017, https://www.youtube.com/watch?v=AosPqLMZnqQ; Collider Videos, "The Room Movie Commentary: Do You Have to Watch It before The Disaster Artist?" YouTube, December 4, 2017, https://www.youtube.com/watch?v=R2dkGHfyLOE; 0816EGG Productions, "The Room Movie Commentary **Fair Use**," YouTube, December 21, 2014, https://www.youtube.com/watch?v=3XZuz-OPMMo; Reel Politik, "The Room (Reel Politik Audio Commentary Track)," SoundCloud, n.d., https://soundcloud.com/reelpolitikpodcast/the-room-reel-politik-audio-commentary-track. One significant omission from the list is a commentary recorded by influential YouTuber the Nostalgia Critic. The Nostalgia Critic commentary, formerly available at https://channelawesome.com/nostalgia-critic-commentary-the-room/, has been scrubbed from the internet and was not available for analysis at the time of this writing.

3. Poniewozik, "All-TIME 100 TV Shows."

4. Hall, "Encoding/Decoding," 128–38.

5. Burke, Permanence and Change, 224–25.

"CAN WE PLEASE NOT TALK ABOUT JAMES FRANCO?" 12

HOW THE DISASTER ARTIST *THREATENED* THE ROOM'S *FANBASE*

JOHN DONEGAN

In the winter of 2017, with *The Disaster Artist* movie set to arrive on the scene, longtime fans of *The Room* were apprehensive. Although many feigned excitement, James Franco's project was rapidly encroaching on their turf. This led to a common predicament faced by fan subcultures: whether to celebrate or condemn their text's newfound popularity. While fans so often complain that their favorite film, musical artist, book, or other artistic work is undiscovered, ostensibly overdue recognition from the mainstream does not guarantee fan satisfaction. On the contrary, such acceptance can often have the opposite effect—the cliché "I used to like X, before they got big" readily comes to mind. So, would long-standing fans ultimately celebrate the mainstreaming of *The Room*? Or would they push back?

As Richard McCulloch discovered during his ethnographic work in the UK, fans of *The Room* attend theatrical screenings with friends to strengthen social ties and foster subcultural capital.[1] Although many fans of cult cinema worry about their cherished texts becoming mainstream, McCulloch did not find this to be the case among fans of *The Room*. In fact, *The Room* is supposedly an anomaly from a cult fandom perspective, as the fans McCulloch encountered said they wanted the film to gain more exposure. Reporting on the phenomenon, McCulloch writes, "There seemed to be little anxiety about [*The Room*'s] increasing

12.1 Dave Franco as Greg Sestero (*left*) and James Franco as Tommy Wiseau in the film adaptation of *The Disaster Artist*. © 2017 by Warner Bros./A24.

popularity. Cult film magazines have often promoted the inaccessibility of particular texts as one of the pleasures of the cult scene,[2] but the 'fans' that I spoke to about *The Room* were far more likely to lament its cultural and/or material elusiveness than celebrate it."[3]

To understand whether *The Disaster Artist* would be embraced by fans for bringing more recognition to *The Room*, as McCulloch's subjects imply, or dilute the existing fandom of *The Room*, University of North Carolina–Chapel Hill instructor Jacob Rhode and I performed quantitative and qualitative analyses of Twitter and Reddit discourse over a four-month period, from November 2017 to March 2018. Nothing about Tommy Wiseau's *The Room* is normal, so it came as little surprise when our results turned out to be quite fascinating.

To be sure, over the past decade and beyond, Wiseau's disasterpiece has flirted with mainstream success on several occasions. In 2009, the film received a particularly big jolt of mainstream media coverage. As Greg Sestero notes in *The Disaster Artist* book, that year "[*The Room*] was featured in *Entertainment Weekly*, *Time*, and *Harper's* and covered on CNN, FOX News, and ABC World News."[4] However, nothing threatened to bring *The Room* into the mainstream as strongly as Franco's decision to take Sestero's book to the big screen. Many fans of *The Room* have supposedly wanted their cult text to reach a larger audience, though this 2017 blockbuster from A24 and Warner Brothers threatened to be a bridge too far. Sure, as McCulloch chronicled, some fans had historically regretted *The Room*'s cultural obscurity, but did they want their beloved text to gain the level of exposure that a Hollywood blockbuster would bring? After four months of analyzing discourse on Reddit and Twitter, we found some recurring topics of concern among fans of *The Room*.

Certain Paratexts Were Privileged over Others

One common topic of discussion was paratexts related to the film, which—unsurprisingly—fans had strong opinions about. During the course of our research, it immediately became clear that certain paratexts were considered to be more authentic than others. Generally speaking, any texts created or explicitly endorsed by Sestero or Wiseau were viewed as valuable; for example, Redditor KryTɪcaL writes, "I would 100% suggest the audio book, it's narrated by [Sestero] and he does his Tommy impression the entire time, it's freaking glorious." On the other hand, anything that undermined or mocked Wiseau was treated with suspicion. Longtime fans of *The Room* were particularly wary of Sandy Schklair's memoir, *Yes, I Directed "The Room": The*

TRUTH about Directing the "Citizen Kane" of Bad Movies. For the most part, fans viewed Schklair's memoir as either revisionist history or a shameless cash grab.

Another recurring point of contention was Franco's failure to provide Wiseau and Sestero with cameos in *The Disaster Artist*. According to the *Hollywood Reporter*, Sestero was supposed to play a casting agent for *Retro Puppet Master*, the real-life B movie he once starred in;[5] however, to the dismay of many, his scene was cut. As Reddit user ObviousSand writes, "I went to a premiere for *The Disaster Artist* a couple of months ago, which Greg Sestero was there doing a Q&A. He said he was a casting agent for *Retro Puppet Master*, [and] the whole RPM part made cutting room floor." Redditor sickofstew commiserates: "How can they do that? They make me sick."

Fans were similarly furious that Wiseau didn't get any screen time. User 19eighties laments, "They couldn't even put Tommy in a movie about his own life. . . . If they were truly creative, they could have figured out a way to make it work in the film. . . . They also completely cut Greg's cameo, so they in a way said they both were not worthy of being in the film. I have to think it would be upsetting in a way since they were being excluded by Hollywood yet again." Theorymeltfool responds, "Damn, Franco et al are even shittier than I thought."

Franco's Condescension

Seeing as some fans of *The Room* have intense parasocial relationships with Wiseau and Sestero, it's perhaps no surprise that many found Franco's project to be condescending and exploitive. To longtime fans, Franco seemed late to the party and not nearly appreciative enough of *The Room* and its stars. We observed several condemnations related to Franco's failure to thank Sestero during a speech at the Golden Globes, and many fans were adamant that Franco took advantage of Wiseau and Sestero.

According to Redditor theorymeltfool, "*The Disaster Artist* feels like a cruel joke/prank on Tommy Wiseau." User allisonauld concurs, writing, "[Franco] has a lot of contempt. Watch them on stage at TIFF [Toronto International Film Festival]. It's on YouTube. He makes a joke about sexual tension between Tommy and Greg. He drapes his arm over Greg's shoulder and leans on Greg like Greg's a statue he just bought." That TIFF speech drew particular ire; articulating a common fan complaint, allisonauld explains, "Tommy was nervous as he was introducing cast members and he asked James a question about something quietly and James says, real loud, 'Don't worry about it, Tommy' with a smirk on his face, like Tommy was a child instead of a colleague. James is a jerk who just saw Tommy's eccentricities as a way to an Oscar."

Concern That Allegations against Franco Could "Trickle into *The Room*"

Amid a series of salacious allegations against Franco around the time that 2018 Oscar nominations were announced, fans became concerned that the history of *The Disaster Artist*'s director could tarnish the legacy of *The Room*. In response to a Reddit thread entitled "I'm just happy for the respect earned by Tommy and the original cast & crew of *The Room* because of the true stories unfold [*sic*] from the book and movie of *The Disaster Artist*," ComaOfSouls writes, "Man I hope so, because now Franco's coming under fire for his past deeds of misconduct, and I worry it might affect the movie, which could trickle into the book and *The Room*." Ultimately, *The Disaster Artist* didn't make a splash at the Oscars, perhaps in part because of the allegations against Franco.

Interestingly, during the four-month period in which we examined the Twitter and Reddit discourse, not much time was devoted to the veracity of the claims made against Franco. This could be due to the nature of *The Room* fandom more generally, which likely skews male. Alternatively, it could be a testament to the type of fans who are active on Twitter and Reddit, which isn't representative of all fans of *The Room*.

Although some have suggested that watching bad films ironically is a uniquely masculine endeavor, this is not true. A recent study found that as many, if not more, women engage in such activities.[6] That said, those who engage in repeat theatrical viewings of cult films have statistically been more likely to be male. Bruce Austin found this to be the case in his study of *The Rocky Horror Picture Show*, as did McCulloch in his work on *The Room*.[7] Nevertheless, the lack of discourse surrounding Franco's #MeToo moment, at least among *The Room* fans on Reddit and Twitter, does lend some credence to the idea that fans of *The Room* are not overly concerned with chauvinistic behavior.

After all, as Sestero points out, *The Room*'s original screenplay is quite misogynistic. "Lisa was a terror: shrill, controlling, greedy, selfish, and vain. She had to be one of the most chauvinistically written characters I'd ever encountered in a script—until, that is, I met her mother, Claudette," he writes in *The Disaster Artist*.[8] And there was some concern that Wiseau himself engaged in questionable behavior on set and during the casting process. Sestero notes, "[Tommy] made no secret of the fact that he was enjoying the physical contact with Juliette, who was obviously suffering between takes. I think half of the guys on the crew had to suppress every chivalrous impulse they had during filming to keep themselves from pulling Tommy off her—especially during the shot in which Tommy appears to be impregnating Lisa's navel."[9] Given these facts, it's not surprising that alleged sexual improprieties *themselves* were not of great concern to fans. Rather, it seems as though they were only highlighted when they had the potential to cast negative light upon *The Room* (as in Franco's case).

Conclusion: *The Disaster Artist* Threatened the Existing Fandom of *The Room*—but Ultimately Bolstered It

We did find some evidence of fans celebrating the mainstreaming of the film, although it was fairly uncommon. As an example, Rob Hill (@BMovieBible, March 21, 2018) posted on Twitter on #WorldPoetryDay, "For over a decade it remained a niche movie, / Exclusively seen by the right on & groovy, / We sat in the dark as Tommy danced his bolero, / We called 'oh hi Mark' when we saw @gregsestero. / But now as if some joyous dream, The Room is everywhere, it's gone mainstream." Hill, for one, claimed to embrace the mainstreaming of *The Room* in the aftermath of *The Disaster Artist.*

Nevertheless, most fans were hostile to Franco and *The Disaster Artist.* In a representative subreddit thread entitled "Can we please not talk about James Franco?" theorymeltfool writes, "Franco can go fuck himself. Want to talk about Franco and his group of talentless hack friends?? Go to /r/thedisasterartistfilm. Oh wait that doesn't exist because it's a shit film that *no one* will remember or reference in a few months." Clearly, this Redditor views the fandom of *The Room* as legitimate and *The Disaster Artist*'s fandom as illegitimate. Although some users attempted to differentiate between types of fandoms, ultimately *The Disaster Artist* seemed to pose a significant threat to the fandom of *The Room,* especially for longtime fans.

Hill's Twitter poem celebrated the mainstreaming of *The Room,* and the fans that McCulloch spoke with in the UK said they wanted the film to achieve mainstream success. However, what we found in our study contradicts these positions. Fans may have *said* they wanted the film to go mainstream, but when it actually happened, these fans became defensive, engaged—and increasingly committed to their fandom.

Despite posing a threat, *The Disaster Artist* ultimately strengthened *The Room* fans' subcultural capital in two important ways: (1) regardless of whether or not existing fans of *The Room* used *The Disaster Artist* to differentiate between that film's fandom and their own, *The Disaster Artist* provided fodder for longtime fans to deepen their social ties and engage in fresh discourse with one another, and (2) it positioned existing fans as being in the know long before Franco's film came on the scene. As *The Room* became increasingly mainstream, long-standing fans of *The Room* closed ranks while pushing back on Franco's project and championing Wiseau's allegedly superior text. For them, Franco's film just pointed out to a new generation what old heads already knew: *The Room* is a work of art quite unlike any other.

JOHN DONEGAN is an independent researcher based in Austin, Texas. His research focuses on cultural sociology, taste cultures, and paracinematic film and TV viewership.

Notes

1. McCulloch, "'Most People Bring Their Own Spoons.'"
2. Jancovich, "Cult Fictions."
3. McCulloch, "'Most People Bring Their Own Spoons.'"
4. Sestero and Bissell, *Disaster Artist*, xv.
5. Ritman, "Story behind Tommy Wiseau's Secret *Disaster Artist* Cameo."
6. Donegan, "'This Is So Bad, We Have to Watch It.'"
7. Austin, "Portrait of a Cult Film Audience"; McCulloch, "'Most People Bring Their Own Spoons.'"
8. Sestero and Bissell, *Disaster Artist*, 227.
9. Sestero and Bissell, *Disaster Artist*, 234.

13 I'M TIRED, I'M WASTED

THE ROOM *AS A WASTE OF TIME*

ERNEST MATHIJS

The Room is a waste of time. Watching *The Room* repeatedly is nothing less than a crime against the sensible and useful spending of leisure time. Why would anyone watch, and watch again, an incoherent story badly acted, painfully incompetent in its execution, backward and dumb in its formal organization, and infantile in its aims and meanings? Well, because *The Room* upsets exhausted impositions that demand that we, the viewers, the participants in culture, *spend time* with some degree of purpose. *The Room* refutes the notion of useful, capitalized time; it counters the idea that meaning and therefore insight can be gained from experiencing it "normally." Instead, it recruits the vilified concept of wasted time and turns it into a middle finger against dictates of how we should devote—that is, *spend*—time with objects and how our time with these objects, in their company, gives value to who we are and how we live. In the case of *The Room,* to waste is not to wither but to prevail in senselessness as an act of resistance.

Johnny's drinking scene sets the tone for the film and its ethos. After he is denied a promotion (time spent usefully without reward), Johnny (Tommy Wiseau) is offered a drink by his fiancée, Lisa. He objects that he does not drink, showing himself once again to be a sensible guy. Lisa insists, however, and after a few drinks of scotchka (a curious mix of scotch and vodka), Johnny is quite drunk—in fact, he seems to get drunk in less than a second, once his lips touch the first glass, but that is just one of many violations of the logical progression of time in *The Room*. Once drunk, Johnny rambles on and deliriously blurts out, "I'm tired, I'm wasted . . . I love you, darling!" The break between the first two parts of the line and the last, a confession, is abrupt, unmotivated, and, while sweet, also totally unnecessary. Is this just a man in the midst of an alcohol-infused ramble? Maybe, but it is also more than just bad writing and acting (and it is *very* bad). In its inadvertent celebration of wastefulness, the line encapsulates the essence of *The Room* and its sudden shifts in delivery and mood, baffling aesthetic tangles, and tangential morsels of drama. The last part of the line lifts up the first two parts. It renders the observational modes of "tired" and "wasted" impressionistic, wise, and poetic—reflecting a heightened feeling instead of a dreary state, a high instead of a low. And then, through sheer incompetence, it drops the ball again and returns to banality.

This chapter acknowledges that the abundance of badness, inconsistencies, and incompetence at display in *The Room* makes it a waste of time, but it also claims that the film, oddly, succeeds in making waste an aesthetic in its own right, through an anarchic act of constant reshuffling that shifts registers so fast, and floats so freely among hysteric, hyperbolic drama and Zen-like calm, that the disorientation it causes becomes its own illuminating compass.

The Room's Many Disorderlies

Before we can make sense of how this compass operates, we need to first review more evidence of the anarchy and disorientation, of the chaos that is *The Room*, as a film and as an example of filmmaking. Instead of just offering a description, let us present a list-like succession of instances that exemplify *The Room*'s wastefulness. According to the chronicle of the film's making, *The Disaster Artist*, the film was shot inefficiently, wastefully, with different and duplicate rigs, sets, and equipment.[1] The story's arc (Johnny is betrayed in his love for Lisa, loses his trust in his friends, and in despair shoots himself) is surrounded by a massive array of improbabilities and irregularities. The film offers no cohesive style, as it shifts from melodrama to bromance, to erotic thriller, to family study, to city symphony (*Let us not forget we are in San Francisco,* say the numerous, repetitive, tracking, and tilting shots of the outdoors). The acting style aims for Marlon Brando and James Dean's method intensity (including the film's most desperate line, "You are tearing me apart, Lisa!") and misses it by a mile. Johnny's circle of friends is nearly impossible to comprehend (is he a pseudo-father to Denny, does he ever really talk to Lisa's mother, and what does her cancer have to do with anything? And who is that new character at the birthday party, and why does he stare like that?).

This essay could easily focus on the relationships between characters (and their sudden appearances and disappearances) and on their motivations (just how long have Johnny and Lisa been engaged, and when is or was their wedding?) to signal how *The Room* fails to merit your time. But let us instead consider the asides: the background elements, such as props, locations, and secondary dialogue. The beginning of the film, when Johnny offers present after present to Lisa (a dress, roses, etc.), offers a treasure trove of such asides. In typical *The Room* fashion, each act of generosity is presented conspicuously to the viewer. But—also in typical *The Room* fashion—these lack any sort of logic or coherence. In the flower shop scene, one of the fastest-paced scenes in the film—in fact, so fast in presenting Johnny as a loving man that it is over before we realize it (therefore shushing the audience)—Johnny enters the shop, orders a dozen roses, is recognized in an offbeat deadpan by the lady at the till, pets a dog, leaves a fat tip, and is showered with compliments (see fig. 13.1). "You're my favorite customer!" shouts the clerk as Johnny rushes out, the entire errand completed in less than twenty seconds. We already knew Johnny was empathy embodied, a truly great man, but what the hell just happened? Too fast to be comprehensible, redundant in content, and bafflingly discombobulated in its execution, the flower shop scene is a masterpiece of waste. Though far from being an egregious example, it is matched in ineptitude by the coffee shop scene, in which Johnny bonds (rebonds?) with his friend Mark. As they line up to place their order, we see all other customers choose the cheesecake (why are we witnessing them placing their orders at all?). But Johnny and Mark pass. Either that cheesecake is the most persistent form of product placement, only to be denied its triumphant climax (Johnny's approval), or it is completely unnecessary. It is the latter, of course. Once seated, Johnny and Mark have nothing to say about cheesecake, opting instead to converse about work and life:

> MARK How was work today?
>
> JOHNNY Oh, pretty good. We got a new client at the bank, we make a lot of money.
>
> MARK What client?
>
> JOHNNY I cannot tell you, it's confidential.
>
> MARK Aw, come on, why not?
>
> JOHNNY No, I can't. Anyway, how is your sex life?
>
> MARK I can't talk about it.
>
> JOHNNY Why not?
>
> SUSAN (the barista) Take your time.
>
> JOHNNY Oh god, I have to run.

In this conversation, it is impossible to discern what is important and what isn't or why, again, Johnny rushes out. As he leaves, he gives Mark a combination high-five, handshake, and fist bump. One of the other customers, who had been in the line at the counter and is now

13.1 Johnny pets the dog at his local flower shop. © 2003 by Wiseau-Films. (Movie still from *The Room*.)

sitting behind Mark, turns around and lifts his fist. He surely wants to fist bump Johnny too, or maybe not? It's impossible to tell; the whole scene has no function in the story, nor does it fuel character development. We already knew about Johnny's work ethic and Mark's amorous complications. It is a succession of loose ends, dialogue that is neither foregrounded nor reduced to background noise, and a string of beatless comments and insignificant trivia. Much more striking than the incoherence, however, is the quick shuffle in the mood: from job chat to intimate inquiries, and then nothing, just a "gotta go."

Moments such as these abound in *The Room*: the curious, overly cutesy pillow/broom fight between pals Michelle and Lisa that gets cut short; Denny's abrupt and impulsive entrances at the door (he can never stay longer than twenty seconds, it seems); the football tossed between friends in the back alley (between waste bins!); the inexplicable appearance of tuxedos, which are never seen again (was that Johnny's wedding rehearsal?); and infinite off-the-cuff comments about long-term relationships, athleticism and buddy sports, education, sexual violence, therapy, and arrests, all of them thrown around and wasted, never intentionally placed or flagged and never followed up on. Futility all around, to the point where shards of conversations are barely audible. Add to that a waste of emotional ranges, which appear at breakneck speed and then veer right off track. In one famous example, Johnny goes onto the roof of his building, complaining loudly about being falsely accused of hitting Lisa, only to shift gear faster than a race car to greet the hitherto invisible Mark: "Oh, hi Mark." Since nothing else governs *The Room*, by default waste is its reigning arrangement.

Waste and the Cognitive Shuffle

Waste is jarring and comforting. Its mess is equally an annoyance, a source of anxiety, a comfort, and a meditative refuge. Almost always, though, it is seen in a negative light. Since World War II, modernity has been subject to an abundance of efforts, commercially hyped or otherwise, that exist to organize our lives around the management and arrangement of stuff—stuff in our rooms and stuff in our heads. Ever since Western family living embraced the dictate that a single-household property had to be managed as a business—as if it were at the same time a hotel, a restaurant, a hospital, and a furniture store showroom, with all leisure activities neatly organized into defined areas (toolshed, study, playroom)—an industry and a genre of "living well"–focused media has emerged to show us how our lives should be organized. Within this framework, there is no room for waste. Morally, waste is a sin. Thus, getting rid of waste is considered a vital political, economic, and social issue. One only has to look at the rhetoric of austerity, at the global traffic of waste exports (countries dumping, shipping, and selling waste) or waste offsets (budgeting waste control), to confirm this. Culturally, waste is the thorn in the side of management psychology: it is reviled by productivity consultants such as David Allen (*Getting Things Done*), household-organization guru Marie Kondo (*Spark Joy, The Life-Changing Magic of Tidying Up*), and pretty much any author of a self-proclaimed feng shui bible. At the same time, waste has its proponents, who see it as a laboratory of creativity (insert your Einstein cluttered-desk quote here). Even then, though, waste is only tolerated with modesty and in moderation. One is allowed to get tipsy only once in a while, not wasted all the time (in spite of Stephen King, Jackson Pollock, Amy Winehouse, or Anthony Bourdain). Throughout, protocols of "civil" behavior have to be maintained, politesse observed. Above all, waste is to be overcome—in real life and even in *The Room*, which despite its colossal time wasting still has pretensions of coming out against wasteful conduct. Right after one of *The Room*'s most indicative moments, just as Johnny has yelled his famous, wasteful line "You are tearing me apart, Lisa!" and Lisa retreats to her room, worried and angry, he adds, as he folds his hands behind his head, "Don't worry about it, I still love you." You see, even Tommy Wiseau wants to move away from waste, on occasion—though the accompanying gesture ill fits the line, creating yet another mismatch (wasted connection?) in an inexhaustible list of them.

In art and entertainment, a continuous battle rages between austerity and wastefulness, be it in the design of comic books and *bandes dessinées* (Franco-Belgian comics; the *ligne claire* ["clear line"] style, popularized by Hergé, is one example), in the animosity toward modern architecture, in visual arts (abstract expressionism versus pop art), or in music (a wall of sound versus minimalist jazz). Tom Wolfe wove a microhistory of aesthetics on the distinction between straight clean and messy curved into *The Painted Word* (1975).[2] True, Miguel de Cervantes's *Don Quixote*; Thomas Pynchon's *Gravity's Rainbow* (which connects entropy to the waste of World War II); Patrick Modiano's messy, lingering interiors of memory and streets of wartime Paris in *Ring Roads*; and William S. Burroughs's wasted hallucinations of *Naked Lunch* make an argument in favor of waste; Don DeLillo tellingly devotes a whole chapter to it in *Underworld*. But they remain minority voices. From reality TV shows about hoarding and storage to well-publicized well-being programs and YouTubers' expertly designed gaming desks, the prevailing message is that waste is bad.

Very few films concern themselves with explorations of waste, and the occasional documentary that wanders near it immediately lifts its nose: it is something to be frowned upon. Still, if one looks a little more closely, waste is important. It offers the chance for films to avoid stringency and steer clear from narrow-minded, laser-focused, unilateral determination. Waste celebrates hesitation, confusion, ambiguity, and transgression. Waste informs the dense scenery of *Blade Runner* and *Casablanca*, with its multilingual, multifaceted, multicultural universe of refugees and runaways, of emotional wanderers and hopeless romantics. Neither Deckard in *Blade Runner* or Rick in *Casablanca* have a purpose; they each had one and lost it. Their actions are explained by others: "You're a sentimental," says Captain Renault (Claude Rains); "like tears in the rain," says Roy Batty (Rutger Hauer), as if completing the sentence. Deckard and Rick know their actions don't "amount to a hill of beans in this crazy world." They know their time is wasted. As Umberto Eco and Scott Bukatman have noticed, *Casablanca* and *Blade Runner* trigger what psychologists call a "cognitive shuffle."[3] These

13.2 Greg Sestero, line producer. © 2003 by Wiseau-Films. (Movie still from *The Room*.)

shuffles, Luc Beaudoin explains, constantly rearrange thoughts, constantly shift, jump, and lapse, and through their continually unfinished haphazardness, through their *aleatory uncertainty* as well their ineptness (a hint of a thought not even worth following far), they reshuffle everyday experiences and therefore reframe them, offering new, albeit blurry, horizons.[4] If you want to sleep, you have to "waste" time by emptying it of meaning-seeking impulses (rationales, lists, worries, wishes, plans). In the waking world, watching *The Room* will do the same for you, guaranteed.

More even than a cognitive shuffle, though, *The Room* is an extension, an application, perhaps, of a purposeless and instinctive being-together that revels in small talk, phatic rituals and repetitive tics, breaks, shifts in focus, lapses in attention, hesitations, drifts, interrupted trains of thought and communication, and divergences that typify what French sociologists Michel Maffesoli and Jean-Luc Nancy independently of each other have described as a sociality, an ambience, an inoperative community.[5] One can find it in cafés (or gin joints in *Casablanca*), social get-togethers, bump-intos and hangouts, waiting rooms, rooftops, and other informal settings that allow (and sometimes stimulate) communication without demanding a purpose or usefulness but that may also play host to occasions anticipated as pleasurable (a party, an event, a meeting with friends). Such an ambience is not necessarily planned and may emerge spontaneously and therefore even be quasi-somnambulist and partially noncognizant—pre-thought. Compare it to that stage right before sleep, similar to the one Beaudoin's cognitive shuffle aims for, in which sleep is about to set in but consciousness has not yet fully switched off. It is a state of ramble, haze, in which time is no longer linear: a heightened moment that is also a waste of time.

Waste, Cult Cinema, and Surplus Effort

As a shuffle of accepted filmmaking practices, as a ruffled aesthetic arrangement, and as a resistance against socioeconomic and moral pressures, waste in the hands of *The Room* becomes a weapon. In the film, that weapon is used accidentally, without intent (let us not forget Wiseau wanted to make a good film, planned as a tragedy). *The Room* shares that incidentality with a select club of films: cult cinema.

Blade Runner and *Casablanca,* two previously mentioned examples of wasteful art—incidental, cluttered, and stuffed, leaky even in how narrative arcs and stylistic moods are thrown around yet brilliant in their evocations of despair, grit, and, above all, love—are known as cult films. It is in that corner of culture, in that messy mishmash of loose ends and awkwardly connected wires (like the jumbled cords on the stage at the end of a sweaty rock concert), that *The Room* finds companionship. It shares with these films, and with films such as *Daughters of Darkness* and *Donnie Darko,* a profound imbalance. Outspoken in their desires to make claims and bold in their aesthetic assertions, these films "fail" to put to use effectively, with moderation, in timely order, and within bounds of normativity and morality, characters and stories that can be accepted as "productive" (i.e., having put their time to good use). Some spoilers (another device that offends the proper conduct of time): Rick lets Ilsa go, Deckard is unsure whether he's a cyborg, Donnie dies (or does he?), and Countess Bathory is impaled purely by accident.

The paradigmatic exemplar here is *The Rocky Horror Picture Show,* which revels in unproductive, inefficient, boundless use of time and energy. Its camp aesthetics are so hyperbolic that they defy usefulness. "One, two, three, four, five, six, seven. Why the fuck does he have seven forks?" asks the audience, bewildered as they observe the film's sacrificial dinner. There are many more examples from *Rocky*—a four-way nondialogue among Rocky, Frank, Brad, and Janet not the least of them ("Ugh," says the audience). But *The Room* is the ne plus ultra of the wastefulness of cult. When I wrote that cult cinema challenges the conduct of time and promotes unproductivity,[6] I had yet to come to terms with its profusion in *The Room,* especially since it is so genuinely unintended.

For Andrew Ross, such waste is a sign of a surplus effort: an attempt to infuse reshuffled meaning in otherwise meaningless imagery and action—a little like an anxious attempt to import a "teachable moment" into a stumble or pratfall. On the audience's part, such surplus effort is a labor of love, a love that is reciprocated through repeat viewing (the ultimate waste of time) and repeating dialogue (resaying nonsense, thus adding further nonsense). But as an insubordination to the command to offer meaning-as-designed, it is a stubborn act of defiance, a firm no to impositions and dictates from civil society and the bourgeoisie (to borrow some militant lingo). It is no surprise that Ross sees surplus efforts at work (!) a lot in exploitation cinema, and in sexploitation in particular.[7] Here too, *The Room* exemplifies the matter. The film's first thirty or so minutes show three elaborate sex scenes (with clichés lifted from virtually every 1990s late-night cable TV erotic drama/thriller—again, unproductivity in action). *The Room* even uses repeat shots of candles, flowing water, and soft-focus sheers in some of the scenes, plagiarizing itself while in the middle of the act itself. Does it matter that the rain flowing from the glass does not match any weather condition suggested outside the room where Johnny and Lisa are having sex? The notion of waste, in other words, is essential to cult cinema: it is a welcome and wildly celebrated reprieve in the face of an efficiency-driven culture that requires returns to be maximized and that demands that our affiliations and emotional spending "deliver" profitable outcomes. It is hopeless to ask of *The Room* what you get out of it. So add something equally wasteful instead: throw a spoon.

Conclusion: There Is No Spoon

One of the most iconic elements of *The Room*'s cult reception is the throwing of spoons, plastic, single-use-only disposable picnic spoons, exactly the kind of utensil sensible societies are banning—an emblem of waste. The spoons first emerged as a reaction to a cognitive shuffle: viewers of *The Room* noticed that interior scenes featured odd props and decorations, like frames of spoons. Normally, a scene's background gives a hint to the characters' moods—it helps us read them. Not here. The spoons just cause confusion and bewilderment because they interrupt and distract. So, in frustration with such waste, someone threw a plastic spoon at the screen. Many others followed, and spoon throwing has become a common ritual during screenings of *The Room*. Right before a screening, I tell my students that the spoons symbolize waste and that they are about to waste their time.[8] I also tell them that while engaging in the wasteful experience of physically launching a representative of waste into the classroom, they might simultaneously find empowerment in rejecting a whole bunch of sensitivities and that some other possibilities to *make meaning* may even emerge (make meaning, rather than find meaning, a surplus effort). When I screen *The Room* for my students, a few thousand of these spoons are thrown around. As they sparkle in the beam of the projector, they create quite the sight. Poetically speaking, they are a glittering sprinkling of cutlery, a shower of clutter. And they are utterly wasteful. My students are good at cleaning up, but every time, a mess remains, like the aftermath of a party. That is the point of *The Room* in a classroom: to upset the strict organization of useful, responsible, teachable time, to offer to all that straitjacketed and cordoned regime of instruction the reprieve of an unstructured yet illuminating afterthought. For that kind of ambience, *The Room* works perfectly. Students go away changed, even if only for an immeasurably short time.

It is mostly an illusion, of course; it is still only a movie. Or, per the famous line from *The Matrix*, which reveals that all representations and appearances of reality are equally useless and wasteful: "There is no spoon."

ERNEST MATHIJS is Professor of Cinema and Media Studies at the University of British Columbia. He is author of *Lord of the Rings: Popular Culture in Global Context*; of *John Fawcett's Ginger Snaps*; and, with Jamie Sexton, of *Cult Cinema: An Introduction*. He is editor, with Jamie Sexton, of *The Routledge Companion to Cult Cinema* and, with Xavier Mendik, of *100 Cult Films*.

Notes

1. Sestero and Bissell, *Disaster Artist*.
2. Wolfe, *Painted Word*.
3. Eco, "*Casablanca*"; Bukatman, *Blade Runner*.
4. Beaudoin, "Discontinuities."
5. Maffesoli, *Time of the Tribes*; Nancy, *Inoperative Community*.
6. Mathijs, "Time Wasted."
7. Ross, *No Respect*.
8. I first screened *The Room* in class in 2008, and I have done so each year since.

PART V
CONSTRUCTING TOMMY WISEAU

OH MAN, I JUST CAN'T FIGURE YOU OUT 14

BUILDING THE PERSONA OF TOMMY WISEAU THROUGH THE DISASTER ARTIST

HARIO SATRIO PRIAMBODHO

> *The Disaster Artist* makes *The Room* more mainstream than *The Room* itself. And probably a lot of people have seen *The Disaster Artist* as well and never go see *The Room* and others that see *The Disaster Artist* actually see *The Room* . . . and I think that's a good thing.[1]
>
> —Danish media researcher, forty-three years old

In its focus on Tommy Wiseau, Franco's *The Disaster Artist* was not Hollywood's first attempt to portray an industry outsider who did not conform to the standards set by their peers. Films such as *Ed Wood*, *Man on the Moon*, and *Auto Focus* have also tackled the tale of the beleaguered entertainment figure who faces down their personal demons and navigates the merciless entertainment-industry power structure. Whether out of amusement, pity, self-recognition, or something else, Hollywood seems to have a soft spot for inscrutable men on the margins whose labor and passion were not fully appreciated from the very beginning.

Within this subgenre, *Ed Wood*, arguably the most famous of the bunch, has the most parallels with *The Disaster Artist* in terms of narrative and style. In the former movie, the director of so-good-it's-bad classics like *Plan 9 from Outer Space* is shown as a sympathetic character who has visions—or, one could reasonably argue, delusions—of grandeur and ambitions of being an acclaimed director in Hollywood, much like Wiseau in *The Disaster Artist*. As well, a major plot point of both films involves the main character's attempt to gain a trusted confidante (Greg Sestero in Wiseau's case and Bela Lugosi in Wood's) as they navigate the treacherous waters of filmmaking. Furthermore, *Ed Wood* seemingly influenced the framing of several comedic scenes in *The Disaster Artist*. Take, for example, when Burton portrays the titular Wood as he tries to direct the blocky and disjointed graveyard investigation scenes of *Plan 9* (see fig. 14.1), and when Bela Lugosi whips Tor Johnson in the laboratory in the making of *Bride of the Monster*. In each scene, Burton depicts Wood as completely oblivious to the importance of multiple takes in making a movie (and many other elements of moviemaking). These segments parallel the flurry of behind-the-scenes portrayals in *The Disaster Artist* of *The Room*'s most infamous moments, like the rooftop scene ("I did not hit her. . . . I did naaaht!") or the unsavory belly button sex scene, in which Johnny appears ignorant of the technicalities of male-female intimacy. Additionally, the last part of both biopics features the respective auteurs attending the premiere of the films that will later be remembered as their magna opera.

The most important legacy of these films, however, is much deeper—and much more personal. In introducing each main "character" to a mass audience previously unfamiliar with him or his strange body of work, these highly acclaimed biopics have had an enormous influence on how the public understands and defines Wiseau and Wood. Accurate or not, *Ed Wood* and *The Disaster Artist* have profoundly shaped people's perceptions of both industry outsiders. In the case of Wiseau, Franco's film reinforces the notion that Wiseau is *as weird* as some people make him out to be, but at the same time leaves enough room for people to speculate (often wildly) about Wiseau's real-life personality.

My first interaction with the figure known as Tommy Wiseau began in New York City around 2007. I had been doing my undergraduate

14.1 Ed Wood (Johnny Depp) is outraged when his directorial prerogatives are questioned during filming of the graveyard scene in *Plan 9 from Outer Space* in Tim Burton's *Ed Wood*. © 1994 by Touchstone Pictures. (Movie still from *Ed Wood*.)

studies in Indiana and was visiting friends when we stumbled on a screening of *The Room* in the East Village. As clichéd as it may sound, that one screening proved to be life changing. Quotes from the movie, such as "I did naaaht" and "Let's ditch this creep," have permeated my wife's and my lexicon on an almost daily basis. Over the years, I have also organized small screenings of *The Room* a few times with friends from different circles. But the most pronounced influence it had on me was that it set off my interest in becoming a researcher within the field of cult films and cult media.

Ever since that first night, I have been trying—often in vain—to answer a simple question: Who the hell is this guy, this person who had the audacity to create something as jarring as *The Room*?

Early on in my quest to find out, I drove two hours north to Chicago multiple times a month, for five months (!), to catch midnight screenings of *The Room* at the Music Box Theatre, bringing several college buddies along for the events. On my first night at the theater, I physically encountered Tommy and Greg for the first time (it certainly wouldn't be the last). I remember feeling so giddy when I saw Tommy walk into the theater; I thought to myself, "He's real, and he's an actual person." In the limited number of interactions I had with him, he always maintained a facade of mystery. One of my friends asked him straight up where he's from, only to get a reply along the lines of, "I'm from the world, I am from everywhere, *ah ha ha*." Not a lot of answers were found that night, least of all from Tommy. *The Room* soon became an obsession, and one that followed me halfway around the world to Sweden, where I am doing my PhD in media studies, inspired in part by *The Room*. Prior to the COVID-19 pandemic, I regularly attended annual screenings of *The Room* at Biograf Spegeln, one of Malmö's art house theaters, where Greg (but not Tommy) would always attend.

In subsequent years, I've found myself going in and out of online forums, scouring different social media platforms, and watching YouTube videos for hours, all in an attempt to piece together some sort of coherent identity for Wiseau. To this day, the picture is still not complete, even with the release of *The Disaster Artist* book and film, both of which offer the most intimate and detailed view of *The Room*'s enigmatic creator among countless news articles and the online resources just mentioned. Despite this, I believe both—but especially the movie, which has had a much wider reach—still have much to offer those interested in unlocking the riddle of Tommy Wiseau, even if it's ultimately unanswerable. The quote that opens this chapter, which was lifted from research I conducted on audiences of *The Room* in 2017 and 2018 in the greater Öresund region (an area comprising Southwest Sweden and parts of

Denmark, including Copenhagen), illustrates the impact *The Disaster Artist* had on both fans and nonfans of *The Room* around the world. That being the case, *The Disaster Artist* is as good a starting point as any if we are to delve into how the screen adaptation of the book helped launch *The Room*—and, just as importantly, its mercurial auteur-creator—into the pop culture nexus.

Right from the beginning, *The Disaster Artist* sets the stage for its audience to ask questions about who Tommy Wiseau is. It features Hollywood heavyweights such as Kevin Smith and J. J. Abrams, among others, being themselves and talking, documentary style, into the camera as they elaborate on their experiences watching *The Room* and reflect on how they perceive Wiseau. Aesthetically, it's slightly unusual to integrate this type of nonfiction storytelling style as a prologue. But it serves a strong purpose, which is to perpetuate the mythology of Wiseau by alluding to the fact that not even these established Hollywood insiders can pinpoint who he really is and how *The Room* came to be. Is he the best director in the world? Is he a misunderstood genius? Or is he just the world's best example of how, once in a blue moon, stars (in an astronomical sense) perfectly align, allowing someone like Tommy Wiseau to seize the opportunity of a lifetime? Meaning, maybe he was just damn lucky.

All of these questions are made possible because of the uncertainties of Wiseau's background. For most of us, knowing a person's origins, age, and other basic biographical details provides critical context that helps us get an image of who that person really is. In Wiseau's case, however, these details are absent or rumored, at best. In other words, without any fundamental information to hang on to, we really can't generate a stable image of Tommy Wiseau. Because of the inconsistent information about Wiseau's background, people's perceptions of him are simply confounded. As one of my interviewees pointed out, "You ascribe Tommy Wiseau attributes that simply aren't there because that's the only way to make sense of it" (Swedish student, twenty-seven years old).[2]

In *The Disaster Artist*, these gaps in knowledge are the source of key moments of tension. For instance, when Dave Franco's Greg Sestero is about to leave his Bay Area home for Los Angeles with Wiseau, his mother confronts Wiseau by asking him his age, to which Wiseau casually, and completely improbably, replies, "Don't worry, I'm Greg's age." Or consider the few times in the film that "New Orleans" is floated as the city where Tommy is from—at least, by Tommy himself—despite his unplaceable, non–New Orleanian accent. It may be that Tommy came from the bayou, but he could also be from Poznań, Poland (as it says on his IMDb page, which was updated shortly after the release of *The Disaster Artist*). Indeed, a great deal of attention in the biopic was put on Tommy's perceived foreignness: his way of speaking; his supposed love for football despite his inability to throw one properly; and odd lines such as, "We make American movie with American discount," uttered when he and Greg are shopping for film cameras. Audiences, especially Americans, would notice the nuances of Tommy's behavior that do not mesh with their own understanding and experience of American culture. Hence his foreignness is overwhelmingly established but never technically confirmed.

The film's depiction of Wiseau as naive and sincere to a fault—a classic underdog, much like Wood in Burton's telling—is another essential building block of his mythology. The belief that Wiseau is 100 percent authentic is inextricable to that mythology; without it, the persona of Tommy Wiseau would utterly collapse. Consider the end of *The Disaster Artist*, when Wiseau, Sestero, and their fellow castmates are attending the premiere of *The Room*. During the climactic event, the audience, incredulous and completely dumbfounded by what they are seeing, laughs at *The Room*, denying Wiseau the satisfaction of having others recognize the riveting, heartfelt drama he worked toward. Unsurprisingly, his reaction is complete disappointment. After a brief reassurance from Greg in the theater lobby, though, the movie suggests that something clicks in Tommy's mind, and when he gets up to speak to the moviegoers after the premiere ends, he says, "I'm glad you liked my comedic movie. Exactly how intended." Even if Tommy was trying to push this new narrative—something that he still occasionally does today—audiences believe they can discern his true intentions. "I heard some people saying that maybe this was his great plan all along. But I don't think so, like I don't want to think so," said one of my interviewees (Danish social media manager, twenty-nine years old).[3] The stakes are simply too high for thinking otherwise. Doing anything less than putting Tommy on a pedestal as a clueless, uncompromising director simply takes the magic and fun out of *The Room* and its eccentric creator.

The idea of the sincere filmmaker is often central to a film being bestowed with the cult label, and it is no different with Tommy and *The Room*. *The Disaster Artist* clearly absorbed this romantic notion, and it shows in its critical but ultimately generous portrayal of Wiseau. This positioning of Wiseau as a kind of strange but harmless antihero helps explain why *The Room* has managed to garner such a big cult following—and, with the success of *The Disaster Artist*, a not-insignificant mainstream one. It's anchored in the idea that Tommy is a filmmaker who failed (badly) at being serious, to channel Susan Sontag. In her famous essay "Notes on 'Camp,'" Sontag expresses her belief that a specific kind of entertainment and pleasure can be found in things that contain a "proper mixture of the exaggerated, the fantastic, the passionate, and the naïve."[4] In the case of *The Room*, failing at being serious is without a doubt a recipe for hilarity and all its pleasures. Add to this the mysteries surrounding Wiseau's personal story, and we have a truly one-of-a-kind phenomenon.

On the other hand, one aspect of Wiseau's persona that isn't ambiguous in *The Disaster Artist* is his disposition toward women. In the film he's depicted as having a general disrespect or lack of understanding of them, a trait that eventually manifests itself in severe displays of jealousy (cases in point: Tommy's attitude toward Greg's then girlfriend Amber and his treatment of Juliette Danielle as Lisa). Without a doubt, the belief that Tommy has, to put it mildly, women issues is taken for granted among viewers and fans of *The Room* and *The Disaster Artist*. In one of my encounters with Greg in Malmö, another person in my group asked him "what the deal is with Tommy and women." To which Greg replied something along the lines of, "He doesn't understand women at all." On a related note, one of my interviewees quipped that he thinks Tommy was scorned by multiple women in his lifetime; this same person thought the dynamics surrounding Wiseau's decision to make a woman the "villain" and his lack of perceived sensitivity in writing female characters are rather "problematic" (Danish research assistant, thirty years old).[5] A different interviewee corroborated this by saying that the "male gaze" becomes even more glaring when you watch *The Room* repeatedly (American content manager, twenty-five years old).[6]

The Disaster Artist certainly fuels the perception that Tommy is completely ignorant when it comes to gender relations and that he does not care about any of the women around him. Crucially, however, it does not offer any clarity—or really even speculation—as to the reasons Wiseau holds the viewpoints he does (or did). Therefore, the question, the mystery, of Tommy's past experiences with women and the reasons he acts a certain way is inserted into the sprawling tapestry of Tommy's myth and persona.

The Disaster Artist gives these kinds of questions back to the audience. Franco's film attempts to provide *some* clarity, but it may fall short. The persona of Tommy Wiseau boils down to what audiences actually believe; the film allows those who may not have done their own sleuthing to get in on the conversation about the mystery of Tommy's life. As such, the myth of Tommy Wiseau is constructed as a byproduct of what people are saying to one another, what they are reading online, and how they pick and choose which tidbits they believe in based on their own perceptions and understandings. Parts of Tommy's tapestry are endowed with meaning that is intricately linked to his persona on- and off-screen. And because the tapestry is a jumbled-up mess, much like *The Room*, audiences can latch on to a number (or just one) of its fraying, disjointed threads,[7] deconstructing and then reconstructing them on the basis of their individual knowledge and understanding, in an endless cycle that—much like a fresh viewing of *The Room*—brings up something new, beautiful, or terrible each and every time.

HARIO SATRIO PRIAMBODHO is Doctoral Researcher at Lund University.

Notes

1. Priambodho, "'Mother of All Bad Movies.'"
2. Priambodho, "'Mother of All Bad Movies.'"
3. Priambodho, "'Mother of All Bad Movies.'"
4. Sontag, "Notes on 'Camp,'" 283.
5. Priambodho, "'Mother of All Bad Movies.'"
6. Priambodho, "'Mother of All Bad Movies.'"
7. Eco, "*Casablanca*."

15 I'M AN AMERICAN, JUST LIKE YOU

THE ROOM *AND AMERICAN CINEMA, IDENTITY, AND MASCULINITY*

LANDON PALMER

From the idiosyncratic filmography of Ed Wood to Hollywood disasters like *The Wicker Man* (2006) to curious cult objects like *Troll 2*, "great-bad" movies have, for decades, attracted the attention of audiences in search of something different. Public interest in such films has arisen from their designation by audiences as so "bad," so off the mark from what they ostensibly intended to be, that they become inadvertently entertaining by the specific ways in which they seem to miss their target. Because their value lies in this perceived gap between intention and execution, the production histories behind such films have grown into a shared source of interest alongside the films themselves, as evinced by the lauded biopic *Ed Wood* and the *Troll 2* documentary *Best Worst Movie*. Through detailed dissections of their histories via films, blogs, and books, patterns emerge as to how great-bad films typically come into being: namely, from creative conflicts between producers and talent, misguided attempts at earning a cheap dollar, or earnest efforts at high-concept ideas executed on a shoestring budget.

What separates *The Room* from the history of such movies is that at one time the circumstances of its making seemed unable to exist except as a hypothetical: what if somebody with no evident competence for filmmaking produced—and somehow completed—a feature film from an endless well of resources? Well, *The Room* proved that such a question need not go unanswered.

Despite its status as an inadvertent, stand-alone cinematic experiment, however, *The Room* is hardly the only entrant into the genre of self-funded great-bad films. In the early twenty-first century, a surprisingly large slate of accidental works of great-badness made their way into the world. During this period, several wealthy older men, *The Room* creator Tommy Wiseau included, used their considerable resources, and the lowered barriers of access to filmmaking equipment and film audiences brought about by twenty-first-century digital technologies and platforms, to realize pet projects that could never have been completed by established, institutional means.[1]

While Wiseau might be the most prominent example of this particular brand of self-fulfilling auteurism, he is hardly alone. Other men who placed themselves on-screen as "self-made" (and all the mythmaking that this particularly American term permits) filmmaker-stars include writer-star Phil Pitzer, of *Easy Rider: The Ride Back*, and Las Vegas-based real estate agent turned filmmaker Neil Breen, a writer, producer, director, and star of five features as of this writing. The work of Wiseau, Pitzer, and Breen does more than show an unanticipated outcome of the democratization of cinematic media. More interestingly, their work—and all its blissful disregard for conventions of cinematic logic—gives us insight into the strange, self-regarding visions of American identity shared among a cohort of independently wealthy white men.[2] For its own efforts, *The Room* has become something of a twenty-first-century urtext for great-bad movies, an unintentional avant-garde parody of cogent cinematic storytelling as well as a passionate and earnest (if ultimately quite troubling) expression of its director's idea of what makes a movie and a man.

Unlike Pitzer and Breen, Wiseau was not born in the United States, and his work is less overtly "about" America. But Wiseau's intentions in making *The Room*—to publicly establish an image of himself as the embodiment of the midcentury male method actor archetype—illuminates a startling vision of cinematic American masculinity as singularly interpreted by its maker, one that is distinct from his great-bad contemporaries. As with other great-bad films, the cult around *The Room* has led to reception practices and cultural objects that detail the story of its making. Told incrementally across thousands of live screenings and finally collected by *The Room* costar Greg Sestero and journalist Tom Bissell in their book *The Disaster Artist*, the source material for James Franco's 2017 film of the same name, the history of *The Room* has unspooled a complex character study of a man attempting to Americanize himself in the cinematic images of Marlon Brando and James Dean through a project that he financed entirely on his own.[3] In its bizarro realization of the myth of American self-determination, *The Room* was Wiseau's attempt to achieve something that he could not through conventional gatekeepers: legitimate Hollywood fame that put him on the same plane as his silver screen idols.

In short, *The Room* was made to concretize Wiseau's vision of himself. And because he produced the film in a vacuum absent of accountability to producers or other superiors, the twisted melodrama that he ultimately created was an inadvertent glimpse into his singular, contradictory vision of the world in terms of sex, friendship, and domestic American contentment. In this vision, Wiseau decisively separates himself from his notoriously enigmatic origins to depict himself, through a character bearing the all-American moniker of Johnny, as fully immersed in an iconic US city (San Francisco, mostly depicted via a Los Angeles soundstage) and enjoying a life of legitimate upper-middle-class comfort at a vaguely defined banking job, complete with casual bouts of football tossing, tuxedoed or otherwise (see fig. 15.1). *The Room* is both a vision and a product of mythical self-making, financed

15.1 Playing football with the guys. © 2003 by Wiseau-Films. (Movie still from *The Room*.)

through individual capital and designed in full service of promoting its ostensible star. As Sestero and Bissell show, *The Room* fulfilled multiple purposes for Wiseau. In addition to demonstrating his ambitions for Hollywood stardom, the project manifested his personal desires for community, friendship, acceptance, and an image of American success that includes the conspicuous display of personal wealth, fame, and masculine dominance.

The film is also a singular expression of what "serious" American cinema is supposed to sound and look like. As Sestero and Bissell chronicle, Wiseau's infamous line reading of "You're tearing me apart, Lisa!" was his attempt to channel Dean's delivery of "You're tearing me apart!" from *Rebel Without a Cause*. Wiseau's performance in *The Room* exhibits the filmmaker-performer's equation of loud, passionate delivery with "serious" male acting, but without the crucial understanding of context. Sometimes—actually, oftentimes—loudness and passion just aren't appropriate. "Of course this guy loves Brando and Dean, I thought," Sestero writes in *The Disaster Artist*. "They're captivating actors because they know exactly *when* to yell, *when* to floor it. Tommy believed you had to floor it for the duration of every scene."[4] Sestero first witnessed Wiseau's unique interpretation of American dramatic arts during the acting class in which they met, when Wiseau performed the scene from *A Streetcar Named Desire* in which Stanley calls desperately after Stella. According to Sestero, Wiseau could not identify the reason Stanley sought Stella's attention, describing "hysteria" as the character's "objective."[5] For Wiseau, an overt demonstration of emotion in the style of midcentury method actors is itself the signifier of great American male performance. Performance, in this case, is not the externalization of the character's goals and feelings but the exhibition of the actor's greatness. Wiseau's divorce of performance from characterization during the class set the stage for *The Room*'s eventual reception. Sestero recalls fellow acting students "giggl[ing]" in response to Wiseau's *Streetcar* performance, for "everyone in the basement studio knew they had just witnessed one of the most beautifully, chaotically wrong performances they would ever see."[6] Such wrongness—that is, Wiseau's apparent inability to recognize the relationship between form and function in creating coherent dramatic meaning—would extend from Wiseau's acting to his filmmaking.

Narrative cinema has a familiar audiovisual syntax that establishes meaning, a cinematic language that moviegoers learn through conditioning (whether they are aware of it or not) and repetition. It's an obvious idea, and it informs everything as variable as when to use a close-up for the most effective dramatic impact and how to employ an establishing shot to signal a change in time and location. As Bissell points out in an earlier assessment of *The Room*, in which he discusses its endless establishing shots around San Francisco, which exhibit no coherent impression of time and space, "Wiseau understands the placement and required tone of such conventions but not at all their underlying meaning."[7] *The Room* possesses most of the usual signs of cinematic syntax but scrambles their traditional uses in a way that inadvertently deconstructs them. Such scrambling is where much of the film's unintended comedy arises—a recognition of wrongness that has shaped the film's cult reception. From performance to shot types, Wiseau seems to know what the tools of conventional filmmaking look and sound like but not the conventions of meaning that such tools have been designed to standardize. In this way, Wiseau further betrays a unique, canted vision of American narrative cinema.

Not all Hollywood standards were thrown out in the making of the film, however. When it came to gendered power dynamics on set, *The Room* appears to have operated strictly according to well-established norms. Sestero and Bissell chronicle Wiseau's shooting of a love scene between Johnny and Lisa (Juliette Danielle) thusly: "[Tommy] made no secret of the fact that he was enjoying his physical contact with Juliette, who was obviously suffering between takes. I think half the guys in the crew had to suppress every chivalrous impulse they had during filming to keep themselves from pulling Tommy off her—especially during the shot in which Johnny appears to be impregnating Lisa's navel."[8]

As *The Room*'s director, lead actor, and sole producer, Wiseau enjoyed stand-alone power over his cast and crew, power that, according to *The Disaster Artist* book, he regularly abused through spying, misrepresenting the production's funding source(s), and—in this case—ignoring an actress's obvious discomfort with performing a lovemaking scene. According to Sestero and Bissell, Wiseau filmed the scene through endless takes over days on an open, not closed, set. The tenor of this shoot shows up in the finished product, a transparently egocentric set piece resulting in the unintended, cringe-inducing image of a man clearly overpowering a woman—a scene whose ultimate goal was to display Wiseau's body as sexually dominant and virile. Wiseau demonstrated here a treatment of an actress that is (as our post-Weinstein moment has confirmed) consistent with Hollywood practices of using the bodies of aspiring women for the gratification of men, and the crew's reluctance to challenge Wiseau shows how on-set power dynamics allow such abuses to take place.[9] In this respect, Wiseau's notion of how American male power works in Hollywood perhaps has more in common with the norms of the industry to which he aspired than is evident at first glance.

In fact, *The Room* is so complete in establishing this ethos that its (and its author's) obvious misogyny has become an integral part of the cult reception that established the film's great-bad status, with viewers often scoffing at the film's retrograde perspective of women. This is perhaps most evident in the "Oh, hi Mark" rooftop scene, one of the most quoted exchanges in the film, in which Johnny and Mark casually discuss domestic violence and the evilness of women. The striking incongruity between the scene's topic of conversation and its tone becomes the source of its humor. Because of its nearly inconceivable obliviousness, it is arguably the scene most responsible for the film's spread through the underground and its eventual entry into the great-bad canon; within the past decade, the line "Oh, hi Mark" has spawned hundreds of memes and YouTube clips, some with millions of views. But the film's fans have not always kept Wiseau's misogyny at arm's length. As I observed firsthand at a 2011 screening of the film on the campus of Indiana University–Bloomington (with Wiseau and Sestero in attendance), mockery of Lisa's body has, as much as Johnny's, been part of the film's interactive viewing experience, including jeers at her during the aforementioned sex scene and vocal reactions to a twitching muscle in Danielle's neck during Lisa's conversation with Michelle (Robyn Paris). Even though Wiseau's cinematic image of his own masculinity has been a subject of mockery by the film's audiences, his concomitant view of women has had a more complicated relationship to its fanbase. While *The Room*'s cult reception is predicated on viewers distancing themselves from the values, ideas, and intentions conveyed by the film, its audiences' interactive viewing practices do not challenge Wiseau's view of Danielle as a body useful for satisfying a particular cinematic experience. From Wiseau's hysterical yet unspecific cries at Stella during acting class to the role of Lisa in *The Room*, this view of women as props for male performance has been key to Wiseau's hopes of establishing himself as a certain type of American film star.

As recounted in *The Disaster Artist* book and movie, the making of *The Room* is a story of one man's aspirations to assimilate into a Hollywood image of the American male—a fact that, frankly, complicates and layers many aspects of the film that have driven its cult reception, such as Wiseau's conspicuous accent. As Sestero recalls, Wiseau at one point declared during a crew meeting, "'I'm an American, just like you.'" When "the absurdity of this comment was met with some giggling," Wiseau responded, "'American with accent.'"[10] Wiseau's project is as American as Horatio Alger, but it ultimately produced a captivating and at-times disturbing realization of what it seeks to imitate. In the process,

Wiseau accidentally produced an image of American masculinity that, in all its strangeness, is inescapably familiar.

In *Indie: An American Film Culture*, Michael Z. Newman argues that film festivals have created spaces in which independent American films can be considered works of national cinema—that is, films that comment on American life rather than simply exist as American products. He illustrates how the theatrical experiences at prestigious film festivals are central to the formation of an alternative US film marketplace, writing, "So many of the narratives of *auteur* and national cinema 'discoveries' and milestones hinge on festival moments: booing, cheering, prizegiving, recognizing that something new has come to claim its rightful place."[11] With its total deference to Hollywood, *The Room* can hardly be considered a work of American independent cinema–as–national cinema that constitutes Newman's argument (*The Room* was independent in the fact of its production but not in the attitude of its Hollywood-aspiring maker), and the film's place in American cinema culture has existed far from the reputable festival circuit. However, like the festival setting that Newman describes, *The Room* came into renown through an active reception context. When University of Southern California student Michael Rousselet happened on the film during its sparsely attended four-walled 2003 exhibition, he invited his friends to screenings that inaugurated its interactive cult traditions in "recognition" of "something new."[12]

More to the point, *The Room*'s alternative exhibition and reception history effectively render the film a work of independent American cinema. Despite Wiseau's Hollywood aspirations, he brought to the film an outsider's perspective on American cinema and depictions of American identity. I write this not because of Wiseau's mysterious national origins—countless immigrants have created the history of American cinema—but because of the peculiar point of view he brought to light in *The Room*. Like Wiseau's public presentation of himself, *The Room* shows an aching desire to pass as "conventional" but, in doing so, only highlights its strangeness, betraying—against its intention—precisely the fears that its director seeks to hide. In the film's attempts *not* to distinguish itself from Hollywood, and its ensuing failure to conform to ideas about everything from masculine performance to normative cinematic language, *The Room* becomes an inadvertent farce of that which it seeks to imitate, a carnival mirror of male-driven notions of American cinematic "greatness" reflected back to us. In this way, *The Room* provides something altogether different from the decisive statements about America by Wiseau's great-bad contemporaries: an accidental work of American national cinema.

LANDON PALMER is Assistant Professor in the Department of Journalism and Creative Media at the University of Alabama. He is author of *Rock Star/Movie Star: Power and Performance in Cinematic Rock Stardom*.

Notes

1. Adding to its unique reputation, *The Room* is both a digital and analog object, having been shot with both digital and film cameras during a transitional moment in the US movie industry. And the film's cult following initially developed through the more twentieth-century forum of the movie theater. With that said, online discourse helped to make *The Room* into a cult object, something that Wiseau's film shares with his great-bad contemporaries.
2. For a more extensive comparison of Wiseau, Pitzer, and Breen, see Palmer, "American Dream of Middle Aged White Guys Making Bad Movies."
3. Sestero and Bissell, *Disaster Artist*, 44, 55, 76, 84–86, 126.
4. Sestero and Bissell, *Disaster Artist*, 58.
5. Sestero and Bissell, *Disaster Artist*, 44.

6. Sestero and Bissell, *Disaster Artist*, 43.
7. Bissell, "Cinema Crudité," 58–65.
8. Sestero and Bissell, *Disaster Artist*, 234.
9. As I have written elsewhere, the work of Pitzer and Breen shares with Wiseau "odd and sometimes troubling representations of women opposite prodigious men, and . . . priorities in displaying their makers' naked bodies in front of the camera." Palmer, "American Dream of Middle Aged White Guys Making Bad Movies." It is worth noting that the depiction of this incident in *The Disaster Artist* by Franco (who has himself been subject to accusations of sexual misconduct) diminishes the troubling tone of this moment as chronicled in the book.
10. Sestero and Bissell, *Disaster Artist*, 156.
11. Newman, *Indie*, 55.
12. See Collis, "Crazy Cult of *The Room*."

TO ERR IS HUMAN, TO AUTEUR, DIVINE 16

TOMMY WISEAU AS AUTEUR

RENEE MIDDLEMOST

I open at the close.

Two men, dressed in tuxedos, sit side by side in a theater. They could not look more dissimilar—one blond, with all-American good looks, smiling, and the other dark, long-haired, with a stony expression on his white, marble-like face. Other people file in, eventually filling the seats. A film begins to play. The dark-haired man leans forward expectantly, while the blond, sensing the mood of the crowd, covers his face with his hands. The audience begins to laugh. First one or two peals ring out, before the room explodes as one, roaring with laughter. The dark-haired man stands and storms from the theater, mumbling, his blond friend following close behind. In the lobby, the blond comforts him, urging him to "look how much fun they're having." The dark-haired man nods, and at the end of the film, he returns to the theater. With the audience cheering their approval, he takes the stage, proclaiming, "I'm glad you like my comedic movie—exactly how I intended. I have vision for this movie."

This scene, which comes at the climax of *The Disaster Artist*, is in many ways the key to interpreting *The Room* and its enigmatic director, Tommy Wiseau. As this chapter will argue, in the moment described above, where Wiseau reframes his intent for *The Room*—taking it from something to be mocked to a deliberate joke—he also establishes his status as auteur, or sole author. By claiming the auteur role, Wiseau can become the supreme dictator of the film's meaning.

16.1 A young Tommy. *Tommy Wiseau* by Tommy-Wiseau-4. Flickr. Uploaded July 11, 2016. https://www.flickr.com/photos/144919956@N05/27956572920.

The idea of the auteur is decidedly of the past. Auteur theory, and ideas of so-called authorial intent, have lost traction in the Academy, as they do not account for the way that fans are now consuming, remaking, and remixing content. Audience responses to *The Room* as a "bad movie" (as highlighted in the scene above, and the subsequent reception) demonstrate how fan activity has eclipsed Wiseau's intent.[1] This can be seen not only in the ritualized cinema responses that accompany the film but also in the extensive fan art, online discussions, and other internet artifacts (memes, gifs) that support the fannish reading of the film as "bad." As a result, the disjuncture between Wiseau's imagined authorial intent and the audience's derisive reception of the film illustrates a larger point about the death of the author and the rise of the active audience in its place. As I will suggest, Wiseau's ability to claim the role of auteur is instead more sustainable when it comes to his greatest achievement: the maintenance of his own secretive, personal narrative.

Auteur Theory

Auteur theory can be traced back to an article by director Francois Truffaut, "A Certain Tendency in French Cinema," published in *Cahiers du Cinema* in 1954.[2] In it, Truffaut discussed the French proposition "la politique des auteurs"—where the director is the true author of any given film. The concept became more widely spoken of following American film critic Andrew Sarris's 1962 article "Notes on the Auteur Theory." In Sarris's formulation, auteur theory is composed of three features: First is the "technical competence of a director as a criterion of value"; without technical competence, one cannot be an auteur. Second is "the distinguishable personality of the director as a criterion of value." In this, Sarris refers to the development of a distinct aesthetic or thematic style that is unique to that director and that serves "as his signature." Finally, and most importantly when considering Wiseau as an auteur, is Sarris's premise that "auteur theory is concerned with interior meaning.... Interior meaning is extrapolated from the tension between the director's personality and his material."[3]

Of his three conditions, the third has brought Sarris the most critique; after all, how can one truly know the director's personality? The idea of knowing is particularly opaque when that director is Tommy Wiseau, a man whose fame is built largely on the unknowability of his "real" origin story. Nevertheless, film scholars Ernest Mathijs and Jamie Sexton have reflected on the crucial importance of biographical information in promoting an author when their cult auteur status is being established. Cult auteurs are celebrated for illustrating "the idea of a lone, heroic figure battling against the odds to create works that are taken to heart by outsider audiences."[4] The celebratory representation of Wiseau in Franco's *The Disaster Artist*, critic Karen Han contends, could be viewed in this light, as it ignores the troublesome parts of Wiseau's character in favor of an uplifting narrative about the triumph of the underdog.[5]

Although auteur theory gained popularity during the 1950s and 1960s, not everyone was convinced of Sarris's argument. Pauline Kael, film critic for the *New Yorker*, was Sarris's most vehement detractor, and the pair engaged in a long-running feud following her 1963 rebuttal article "Circles and Squares." In a scathing analysis, Kael systematically dismantles Sarris's three criteria, concluding that "auteur theory is a hindrance to clear judgments. . . . It is an insult to an artist to praise his bad work along with his good; it indicates that you are incapable of judging either."[6] In completing her analysis, she contends that auteur theory is most dubious because of its obsession with the "cult of personality."[7] For Kael, this assumes that all art by a director deemed an auteur with a distinct signature is worthwhile. She isn't the only one to cast suspicions on auteur theory, and it is now out of favor within the Academy for numerous reasons, not least of which is its attribution of a sole, unified vision to one person. In most, if not all, modern productions, the final version of any media content is typically a team effort involving multiple rewrites, personnel changes, and revisions after audience review.

In the wake of #MeToo, *New Statesman* film critic Ryan Gilbey writes, the death knell may have sounded not only for the outdated notion that a film is the result of a singular vision but also for the elevation of directors as creative geniuses above reproach. This philosophy, he argues, is increasingly difficult to maintain in the face of evidence and accusations of misdeeds committed by exalted figures such as Roman Polanski, Quentin Tarantino, and Alfred Hitchcock.[8] Although audiences are now aware of the problematic behavior of the above-mentioned men (to name but a few), they may be less aware that their use of auteur status as a cover for allegedly abusive behavior echoes the conduct of Wiseau. In *The Disaster Artist,* we witness a scene where, as Sestero recounts in the book, Wiseau (James Franco) verbally abuses actress Juliette Danielle (Ari Graynor, playing Lisa) for her body shape and skin blemishes while filming a sex scene. When Sestero (Dave Franco) pulls Wiseau aside to rebuke him, Wiseau invokes the behavior of Stanley Kubrick and Hitchcock (particularly his treatment of Tippi Hedren in *The Birds*) to justify his abuse of Danielle.[9] While *The Disaster Artist* serves in many ways to rehabilitate the image of *The Room,* and Wiseau, one cannot help but feel uneasy at Wiseau's treatment of both Danielle and other cast and crew throughout the filming.

Finally, if Wiseau is to be considered an auteur, what would his signature be? Incompetence? Incoherence? Cult appeal? Strange, quotable lines of dialogue? Whatever it is, these assessments of *The Room* appear to be incompatible with how Wiseau imagines himself and his magnum opus. Perhaps, then, we might better understand Wiseau through the insight of poet and filmmaker Jean Cocteau: "The only technique worth having is the technique you invent for yourself."[10] Cocteau's remark encapsulates Wiseau's approach—one in which he *imagines* himself as an auteur, or the sole author of a film produced by his own distinct technique.

While film scholarship may never truly depart from the elevation of the author, scholar Jason Mittell instead proposes "a mode of attribution we might call *authorship by responsibility.*"[11] He clarifies that while a film is created through the labor of many, the director acquires authorship by responsibility—as they ultimately decide what to include in the finished work. Here we may be on firmer ground. Despite the contentious status of auteur theory, and attribution of sole authorship, Tommy

Wiseau's responsibility for the unique vision displayed in *The Room* has never been questioned.

The Talented Mr. Wiseau: Tommy's Inspirations

Iconic directors and writers such as Orson Welles (*Citizen Kane,* 1941) and Tennessee Williams (*A Streetcar Named Desire,* 1941) are also frequently cited as inspirations for Wiseau. Less attention, however, has been paid to the inspiration that Wiseau draws from Anthony Minghella's *The Talented Mr. Ripley,* which might be the most disturbing and yet revealing key to Wiseau's "true self." In *The Disaster Artist* book, Sestero recounts Wiseau's obsession with classic Hollywood, and in particular their shared love of James Dean as a tragic hero. (One chapter recounts a road trip Wiseau and Sestero took to the site of Dean's fatal car crash in the dead of night.) They had spent a lot of time watching films, and during a tense period in their relationship they see *The Talented Mr. Ripley* together. Sestero, having previously viewed it with a friend, and struck by the similarities between the duplicitous Tom Ripley (Matt Damon) and Wiseau, offers the following remark: "I knew precisely why my friend was forcing me to watch it. Tom Ripley is someone who wants to belong to respectable society so deeply that he'll do anything."[12]

Entranced by the film, which they happen to see on the night of the 2000 Golden Globe Awards, Wiseau leaves the theater determined to create his own award-winning film, with Sestero observing: "Not until years later did I really understand what Tommy had done, which was to create his own personal version of the three main *Ripley* characters. This meant he mix-and-matched their characteristics according to his own strange value system, after which he placed them into a warped version of his own life experience. . . . It's such a strange interpretation of the story, but it was what Tommy took away from it. Tommy couldn't see what the film was actually trying to tell him about himself."[13]

Tommy's Constant Reinvention

As I have argued elsewhere, *The Room*'s paratexts, such as Sestero and Bissell's book and Franco's film adaptation, have helped maintain the cult status of *The Room* and provide multiple entry points into *The Room*'s fandom.[14] It is also clear that this cultification process has shifted the focus from *The Room*, the film, to Wiseau, as cult object. Incidents such as Wiseau's ongoing court battle with the makers of the tell-all documentary *A Room Full of Spoons* demonstrate his awareness of this shift, and, as a result, the need to protect his own brand and mystique.[15] So while Wiseau may not be an auteur in the traditional sense of the word, I believe Wiseau *is* one—the auteur or architect of his own story. As collection editor Adam Rosen observed in the *Atlantic*.com, "*The Room* was wildly successful in one important way: putting Tommy Wiseau's singular, unedited vision out into the world."[16] While as an audience we can never be entirely sure of Wiseau's intent for *The Room*, the aforementioned paratexts allow audiences and fans to assume the authenticity of Wiseau's original vision. We can be reasonably certain that the protection of his past—his age, source of wealth, and country of origin (as James Franco dubbed it, the "Holy Trinity")—is Wiseau's way of writing his own story and protecting it from the mockery that *The Room* received.

The climax of *The Disaster Artist* movie, which I narrated in the opening of this essay, is, of course, a revisionist history of audience reception of *The Room*. The acceptance of *The Room* as a cult film was a slow burn, not an instant recuperation and loving embrace by the audience, as Franco's film suggests. In 2003, the initial two-week run of *The Room* (self-funded by Wiseau) at the Laemmle Fairfax and Fallbrook Theatres in Los Angeles was met with audience disbelief (and certainly no cheering), and a large number of patrons demanded refunds on the ticket price. However, word-of-mouth reports about the film began to spread, largely because of the efforts of screenwriter Michael Rousselet, who encouraged friends to attend showings.[17] Reports eventually reached celebrity fans such as Paul Rudd and Kristen Bell, who held their own private screenings,[18] and a DVD was released in December 2005. Although at-home watch parties played a role in increasing the film's popularity, *The Room* is unique in that its cultification is still centered on the shared audience experience of viewing the film in a cinema. In fact, it is perhaps one of the last films with a cult following to maintain the centrality of the cinema experience.

The audience reception, and reading of the film as a comedy, led to Wiseau's gradual rebranding of the film as a black comedy—a claim that *The Disaster Artist* book and film clearly contradict. It is here that Wiseau's power as an auteur, expressed in his ability to rewrite both his own personal history and the reception narrative of *The Room,* is most evident. While audiences can never really know the "truth," Wiseau has proven expertly capable of retconning both narratives to suit his own worldview.

"I Always Wanted to Have My Own Planet. Call It Tommy's Planet. My Planet Will Be Bigger than Everything": Conclusion

This chapter has offered a brief overview of why Tommy Wiseau should be considered a cult auteur. Key literature highlights the conflicting nature of auteur theory with current patterns of audience and media consumption and production and the pitfalls of evaluating a text on the basis of its author's "signature." Yet as I have argued, Wiseau can be considered an auteur for the more substantial work he conducts in the creation of his own narrative. It is the mystery that Wiseau has cultivated by tightly guarding his "Holy Trinity" that ensures he remains the sole author of his own story—and thus ensures the continual cult appeal of *The Room* and subsequent Wiseau projects. Audiences are fascinated by Wiseau and, in turn, his creative output. If Wiseau successfully prevents the release of tell-all documentaries such as *A Room Full of Spoons*, then perhaps his dream of going down in moviemaking history will be fulfilled. Then again, even if he doesn't, fans' willingness to believe in his self-created mythology may immunize them to any new information, no matter how inconvenient. All of which is to say, while Wiseau certainly won't be known as the greatest director of all time, or the one who made the greatest movie, he very well might be the last great cult auteur.

RENEE MIDDLEMOST is Lecturer in Communication and Media at the University of Wollongong. Her work appears in *Celebrity Studies*, *M/C Journal*, and *Australasian Journal of Popular Culture*.

Notes

1. See Barthes, "Death of the Author," 142–48.
2. See Truffaut, "Certain Tendency in French Cinema," 221–37.
3. Sarris, "Notes on the Auteur Theory in 1962," 562.
4. Mathijs and Sexton, *Cult Cinema*, 68.
5. Han, "We May Never Know the Truth behind Tommy Wiseau and *The Room*."
6. Kael, "Circles and Squares," 50.
7. Kael, "Circles and Squares," 51.
8. Gilbey, "End of the Auteur?"
9. See also Han, "We May Never Know the Truth behind Tommy Wiseau and *The Room*."

10. In Kael, "Circles and Squares," 49.

11. Mittell, *Complex TV*, 88.

12. Sestero and Bissell, *Disaster Artist*, 177–78.

13. Sestero and Bissell, *Disaster Artist*, 189.

14. Middlemost, "Renovating *The Room*."

15. RockHaven Pictures/Rick Harper, "This Is Why You Haven't Seen *Room Full of Spoons*... Yet."

16. Rosen, "Should Gloriously Terrible Movies like *The Room* Be Considered 'Outsider Art'?"

17. Jones, "How *The Room* Became the Biggest Cult Film of the Past Decade."

18. Rose, "Is This the Worst Movie Ever Made?"

17 I DON'T HAVE A FRIEND IN THE WORLD

THE LONELY AUTHENTICITY OF TOMMY WISEAU

KEITH KAHN-HARRIS

I met Tommy Wiseau in 2015, before one of the regular screenings of *The Room* at the Prince Charles Cinema in central London. I happened to be first in the queue and arrived before anyone else at the merch stall where Tommy and Greg were going to be meeting and greeting. They weren't quite ready to meet the public, and I stumbled upon an animated conversation between Tommy and someone who might have been his manager, publicist, or gopher (Greg stood quietly to the side).

I never figured out what the conversation was about, but as I looked on, waiting for my chance for a selfie and signature with the great man, I was struck by Tommy repeatedly referring to the venue as the "Charles Prince."

I remember thinking, "That's exactly the kind of mistake Tommy Wiseau would make." It's also the kind of mistake that Johnny in *The Room* would make. I'd had a rare chance to eavesdrop on the Tommy that existed out of the public eye, only to find exactly the kind of strangely twisted English that pervades both his public appearances and his character in his film.

At times, Tommy's mangled English is treated as a function of his foreignness. But, aside from the danger of being both patronizing and even racist, one cannot simply put his mistakes down to Tommy not being a native English speaker. Take the Charles Prince example. There are languages for which this would be an understandable mistake. In

17.1 The marquee at the Prince Charles Cinema. *See Tommy Wiseau Here!* by Louise McLaren. Flickr. Licensed under CC BY 2.0. Taken January 30, 2012. https://www.flickr.com/photos/82437626@N00/6791045869.

Hungarian, for example, Prince Charles would translate as Charles Herceg. The word order is similarly reversed in Japanese and Chinese. But, as far as I am aware, no one has ever claimed that Tommy was born in Hungary, Japan, or China. The most likely suspect remains Poland, where Prince Charles translates to Książę Karol. French, a language Wiseau also acknowledges speaking, translates to Prince Charles exactly. Romania, which is sometimes mentioned as a possible country of origin, translates it to Prințul Charles. In fact, other than Hungarian, all eastern European languages maintain the same word order as English, even non-Slavic ones such as Lithuanian, Latvian, Albanian, and Estonian.

This is not the only Wiseau-ism that cannot be attributed to an imperfect transition from his native language, whatever it might be, to English. The repeated use of *future wife* rather than *fiancée* to describe Lisa in *The Room* does not appear to be simply an awkwardly literal translation from a language in which there is no single word for *fiancée* (and, of course, it could not be a literal translation from French, from which English borrows the word). *Fiancée* in Polish is *narzeczony*; *future wife* in Polish is *przyszła żona*. This distinction is also present in Hungarian (which is similar to other eastern European languages in this respect, in contrast to the Prince Charles anomaly), where *fiancée* is *vőlegény* and *future wife* is *jövőbeli feleség*.

Now, granted, I am making Google Translate do a lot of heavy lifting in this analysis, but I think my contention should be clear: even if we were to assume that Tommy Wiseau grew up speaking the language of an eastern European country (which seems most likely), or even if we were to assume that he is fluent in French, we cannot necessarily attribute his linguistic peculiarities to an imperfect facility with English. Or at the very least, we cannot attribute them to a tendency to refract an unconsciously non-English substrate through English.

We therefore have to acknowledge something that is known to every fan of *The Room* but that is extremely difficult to acknowledge in contemporary critical theory: Tommy Wiseau is uniquely odd. His strangeness cannot be simply traced back to a foundational life trauma or cultural dislocation—although those are surely part of the story—but retains an excess beyond his biographical details. Tommy's oddness may have been exacerbated by his life experience but is not reducible to it.

As a passionate fan of *The Room* and as someone whose intellectual upbringing has been infused by critical theory, I find myself bifurcated here. I am drawn to Tommy and his greatest creation because of his strangeness, his hilarious and bizarre mistakes, and a central performance so peculiar that it seems to stand outside the history of cinema. I see him as someone whose way of looking at the world is so singular that to step into it is to step into a world transformed. And yet I also "know" that none of us is born from nothing. Tommy Wiseau, like anyone else, does not stand outside of time, space, and culture.

The problem here is one of authenticity. This concept represents the point where everyday common sense and critical discourse diverge most alarmingly. We cannot seem to do without the authentic as a way of judging others, ourselves, and, most importantly, culture. The authentic artist remains the gold standard across a swath of fields of cultural production. But it is a concept that has been forensically deconstructed too many times to be sustainable. None of us possesses an internally coherent, consistent, and unitary point of origin that can be articulated (or betrayed) in creating art or anything else. We are performers on a succession of stages, constantly improvising bricoleurs in a world where to be social is to inevitably be compromised.

In some respects, Tommy Wiseau's work can be judged not just as demonstrating his catastrophic failure to achieve a common standard of artistic authenticity but also as revealing the inherent impossibility of treating the concept as the basis for aesthetic standards. Insofar as *The Room* can easily be parsed, it appears at least in part to be an attempt to show, in the character of Johnny, an ideal of authentic American manhood: Johnny is loyal to friends, plays football, is a good employee, is an ideal and faithful "future husband." This idealization is mirrored by Tommy's similarly desperate attempts to be an authentic exemplar of American culture: a Hollywood filmmaker, a maker of American culture, a writer, and an actor. Johnny/Tommy both fail at their attempts. Johnny's modeling of himself on the ideal American male does not prevent him from being betrayed by his "real" American friends and his fiancée. Tommy's desire to be an auteur in the movies is met only with ridicule.

Johnny/Tommy do not simply fail at their twin authenticity projects; those were never possible in the first place. Johnny fails to understand that you can try to be as authentic as you want but that this ultimately makes no difference to how people act toward you. Tommy fails to understand that being an authentic auteur is never simply about taking on and aping the trappings of the filmmaker. Johnny/Tommy are both forced to confront the fact that there are no fixed standards of authenticity that can be achieved through mimesis; the awarding of authentic credibility is carried out in an improvisatory and inconsistent fashion. If you don't have it, you can never get it.

Tommy Wiseau's remarkable second act is, ironically, a testament to the possibilities of authenticity's impossibility. In one respect, his attempt to create an authentically serious movie and to be an authentically serious auteur may have totally failed, but there is always more than one form of authenticity available. What Tommy has in spades is another form of authenticity: *consistency*.

My encounter with him at the Prince Charles Cinema was a demonstration of this consistency. In private conversation, he was Tommy

Wiseau. On the stage doing a Q and A later that evening, he was Tommy Wiseau. In *The Room,* he was Tommy Wiseau. In his various other filmmaking ventures, he has been Tommy Wiseau. And, of course, as Johnny, he was Tommy Wiseau. Indeed, so complete is his Wiseauness that the other characters in *The Room* also talk as peculiarly as he does.

Such consistency is, I think, part of what those of us who love *The Room* and repeatedly pay to get him to sign merchandise are responding to. On the first few times you watch the movie, perhaps you laugh, incredulous with ridicule. Beyond that, much of the appeal seems to lie in the absoluteness of Tommy's consistency. Not only will the film always be the same, but so will Tommy. He dresses the same, talks the same, and never, ever evolves.

There is something almost heroic here. Consistency at this level is not an easy thing to achieve. Tommy would be forgiven for occasionally lashing out, for wanting to be taken seriously some of the time, for demanding we show some respect—but he rarely does. When questioners ask him about something he doesn't want to talk about (like his origins), he simply bats the question away. And even on the rare occasions when he does publicly lose his temper, he does so in a consistently bizarre, Tommy-like way.

People enjoy laughing at *The Room,* but it isn't always clear whether fans are laughing at or with Tommy Wiseau. In fact, it may be that the distinction between *laughing at* and *laughing with* is not sustainable in his case. Rather, I would suggest that our response to him might be better understood as a kind of homage to his strange authenticity. That we laugh may speak volumes about the ultimate impossibility of authenticity as an ideal, aesthetic or otherwise. Tommy represents what a truly authentic, consistent human being would actually look like—and it is risible.

Tommy Wiseau is not the only example of risible authenticity. Over the decades of its existence, heavy metal music and culture has also explored the strange simultaneity of being absolutely authentic and absolutely ridiculous. The American band Manowar is one example of this. With their oiled bare chests, their fur pants, their five-hour concerts, their proud status as "the loudest band in the world," their sloganizing ("All men play on ten!"; "Death to false metal!"; etc.), and their complete and utter seriousness, they are a gift to anyone who considers metal to be a pathetic performance by immature losers who are unaware of how silly they look. And yet metal fans are indeed aware of how ridiculous Manowar are, *and they love them anyway*. The band members, as far as anyone can tell, do take themselves absolutely seriously, but fans are capable of simultaneously appreciating this seriousness and adoring its ultimate silliness.

What Manowar, and Tommy Wiseau, teach us is that if we were to aspire to be absolutely authentic, we would likely be laughable. To be truly authentic in this way requires a kind of self-sacrifice, removing oneself from the possibility of serious aesthetic contemplation to demonstrate what an entirely consistent life would look like. There is something subversive, even transgressive, about this way of being. It punctures the bubble of excessive irony and arch self-awareness that is so commonly associated with the acquisition of cultural capital. To persist, to be consistent when you are constantly being mocked, is to question hierarchies of cultural value, to dare the audience to do its worst, knowing that no insult can ever harm you. Further, this kind of authenticity reveals the constructed hollowness of other ways of being an aesthete; it highlights the performative quality of *cool*. The stakes involved in performing the exaggerated sufferings of the authentically tortured, complex, mercurial auteur are nothing compared to the heroic effort required to be consistently authentic in the Wiseau fashion.

But at what cost? What must it be like to spend your life going around the world being a source of laughter, however affectionate? What must it be like to be repeatedly publicly confronted with the failure of your most personal artistic statement to achieve its stated aims? In some respects, Tommy's singularly authentic strangeness puts him beyond the point where empathy is easy. Again, the absoluteness of his consistency means that to view him from any other standpoint becomes difficult. Most of us live in a messy morass of contradictory incoherence. This is also what protects us from the vulnerability that comes with embracing a life of predictable consistency. To be truly authentic requires removing oneself from the world of compromise, reversal, and nimble contingency. This is, by definition, a lonely and risky path.

I fantasize sometimes that "Tommy Wiseau" will prove to be some kind of performance art project. It may actually be easier to think of the character that way, so unusual is he. To think of Tommy as a pure outgrowth of his essential uniqueness is itself bizarre. Yet we are forced to confront this possibility in the absence of any alternatives. That so little is known of him, despite the efforts of journalists to dig deeper, suggests that, beyond resolving the question of his birthplace, there may be nothing else to know.

Over the years, then, as Tommy grows older and his fans do too, might our laughter become more nervous, fearful even? If the mask never slips, if it proves that there never was a mask in the first place, what might we do with Tommy then? If Tommy is indeed one of the few humans to have achieved absolute authenticity, might we pity him for more than being an incompetent filmmaker? Might our encounters with his living reality become an audience with an other so absolutely unlike us that we can barely imagine its horror?

In fact, Tommy has already shown us what this horror looks like. The ending of *The Room* sees Johnny in a state of inconsolable turmoil as he wails, "I don't have a friend in the world." Throughout the film, Johnny reveals himself to value human connection and friendship above everything else. He constantly repeats that Mark is his best friend, that he loves Lisa, that he takes care of Denny. When it becomes clear that "everyone betray [him]," he has absolutely nothing left that he values (not even the TV, likely the very source of his beloved all-American Hollywood fantasies). While the movie's melodramatic acting, writing, and direction seem to preclude the audience being moved by Johnny's despair, the possible similarities to Tommy's real life might give us pause. The book *The Disaster Artist* portrays Tommy as someone who has known real loneliness and alienation from the world and who is absolutely desperate for the friendship of Greg Sestero, seemingly having few other sources of human connection prior to meeting him.

Tommy's ultimate fate is a happier one than Johnny's (or, in the absence of publicly available information to the contrary, it appears to be that way). He is loved, in a way; he is successful, to an extent; he has made his mark on the world, albeit not quite the way he intended. Yet he remains apart from the world. He, like Johnny, can ape the conventions of the real world, but he is condemned to never really get it. His authenticity means he will always be alone.

Maybe, after fans like me have watched *The Room* repeatedly for years, the laughter will fade away and we will feel the chill of the sadness at its heart. Still, the layers of hilarious oddness are so deeply stacked on top of one another that we may never be able to make that connection with a singularly lonely soul. That is Tommy Wiseau's tragedy, and perhaps it is ours too.

KEITH KAHN-HARRIS is Senior Lecturer at Leo Baeck College; Associate Lecturer at Birkbeck, University of London; and Project Director of the European Jewish Research Archive at the Institute for Jewish Policy Research. He is author of *Strange Hate: Antisemitism, Racism and the Limits of Diversity* and of *Denial: The Unspeakable Truth*. He is editor, with Titus Hjelm and Mark LeVine, of *Heavy Metal: Controversies and Counterculture*.

WORKS CITED

Abrams, Nathan. *Stanley Kubrick: New York Jewish Intellectual*. Brunswick, NJ: Rutgers University Press, 2018.

Adler, Stella. *The Technique of Acting*. New York: Bantam Books, 1988.

Austin, Bruce A. "Portrait of a Cult Film Audience: *The Rocky Horror Picture Show.*" *Journal of Communication* 31, no. 2 (1981): 43–54. https://doi.org/10.1111/j.1460-2466.1981.tb01227.x.

Barthes, Roland. "The Death of the Author." In *Image, Music, Text*. Translated by Stephen Heath, 142–48. London: Fontana, 1977.

Bayliss, Robert. "What Don Quixote Means (Today)." *Comparative Literature Studies* 43, no. 4 (2006): 382–97.

Beaudoin, Luc. "Discontinuities: Love, Art, Mind." Unpublished manuscript, last modified 2017. Leanpub Open Access. https://cogzest.com/books/discontinuities-limerence-art-and-mind/.

Bechdel, Alison. "The Rule." In *Dykes to Watch Out For*, 22. Ithaca, NY: Firebrand Books, 1985. http://bechdeltestfest.com/about/.

Berman, Judy. "The Streaming Void." *The Baffler*, March 2018, no. 38.

Bissell, Tom. "Cinema Crudité: The Mysterious Appeal of the Post-camp Cult Film." *Harper's Magazine*, August 2010.

Bourdieu, Pierre. *Distinction: A Social Critique of the Judgment of Taste*. Translated by Richard Nice. Cambridge, MA: Harvard University Press, 1984.

Brestoff, Richard. *The Great Acting Teachers and Their Methods*. Lyme, NH: Smith and Kraus, 1995. Kindle edition.

Bukatman, Scott. *Blade Runner*. London: British Film Institute Modern Classics/Palgrave, 1997.

Burke, Kenneth. *Permanence and Change: An Anatomy of Purpose*. New York: New Republic, 1935.

——. *The Philosophy of Literary Form: Studies in Symbolic Action*. Baton Rouge: Louisiana State University Press, 1941.

Cervantes, Miguel de Saavedra. *Don Quixote*. Translated by Walter Starkie. New York: Signet Classics, 1965.

——. *Don Quixote*. Translated by Edith Grossman. New York: Ecco, 2003.

Christman, Phil. "The Cinema of Inadvertence, or Why I Like Bad Movies." *Hedgehog Review* 21, no. 3 (Fall 2019). https://hedgehogreview.com/issues/eating-and-being/articles/the-cinema-of-inadvertence-or-why-i-like-bad-movies.

Cocks, Geoffrey. *The Wolf at the Door: Stanley Kubrick, History, and the Holocaust*. New York: Peter Lang, 2004.

Cohn, Ruby. "The World of Harold Pinter." *Tulane Drama Review* 6, no. 3 (March 1962): 55–68. https://doi.org/10.2307/1124935.

Collis, Clark. "The Crazy Cult of *The Room*." *Entertainment Weekly*, December 12, 2008. https://ew.com/article/2008/12/12/crazy-cult-room/.

Craig, Rob. *Ed Wood, Mad Genius: A Critical Study of the Films*. Jefferson, NC: McFarland, 2009.

Deleuze, Gilles. *Cinema II*. New York: A&C Black, 2005.

Donegan, John. "'This Is So Bad, We Have to Watch It': Acquiring Subcultural Capital through Oppositional Viewing Strategies." In *Consumer Identities: Agency, Media, and Digital Culture*, edited by Candice D. Roberts and Myles Ethan Lascity, 95–109. Bristol, UK: Intellect Ltd, 2019.

Donnelly, Kevin J. *The Shining*. New York: Wallflower Press, 2018.

Durán, Manuel, and Fay R. Rogg. "Constructing Don Quixote." In *Fighting Windmills: Encounters with Don Quixote*, 57–81. New Haven, CT: Yale University Press, 2006.

Dyck, John, and Matt Johnson. "Appreciating Bad Art." *Journal of Value Inquiry* 51 (2017): 279–92.

Dyer, Richard. *Only Entertainment*. 2nd ed. Abingdon, UK: Routledge, 1992.

Eco, Umberto. "*Casablanca*: Cult Movies and Intertextual Collage." *SubStance* 14, no. 2 (1985): 3–12. https://doi.org/10.2307/3685047.

Gilbey, Ryan. "The End of the Auteur?" *Guardian*, March 23, 2018. https://www.theguardian.com/film/2018/mar/23/the-end-of-the-auteur.

Hall, Stuart. "Encoding/Decoding." In *Culture, Media, Language*, edited by Stuart Hall, Dorothy Hobson, Andrew Lowe, and Paul Willis, 128–38. London: Hutchinson, 1980.

Han, Karen. "We May Never Know the Truth behind Tommy Wiseau and *The Room*." *Vice*, December 18, 2017. https://www.vice.com/en_au/article/yw5g95/the-disaster-artist-tommy-wiseau-reality-essay.

Holmes, Theodore. "Don Quixote and Modern Man." *Sewanee Review* 78, no. 1 (1970): 40–59.

Hunter, I. Q. *Cult Film as a Guide to Life: Fandom, Adaptation, and Identity*. New York: Bloomsbury, 2013.

Jancovich, Mark. "Cult Fictions: Cult Movies, Subcultural Capital and the Production of Cultural Distinctions." *Cultural Studies* 16, no. 2 (March 2001): 306–22. https://doi.org/10.1080/09502380110107607.

Jones, Nate. "How *The Room* Became the Biggest Cult Film of the Past Decade." *Vulture*, June 27, 2013. https://www.vulture.com/2013/06/the-room-10th-anniversary-history.html.

Kael, Pauline. "Circles and Squares." *Film Quarterly* 16, no. 3 (Spring 1963): 12–26. https://doi.org/10.2307/1210726.

Kolker, Robert, and Nathan Abrams. *Eyes Wide Shut: Stanley Kubrick and the Making of His Final Film*. New York: Oxford University Press, 2019.

MacDowell, James, and James Zborowski. "The Aesthetics of 'So Bad It's Good': Value, Intention, and *The Room*." *Intensities*, Autumn/Winter 2013, 1–30. https://intensitiescultmedia.files.wordpress.com/2014/01/j-macdowell-j-zborowski-the-aesthetics-of-so-bad-its-good1.pdf.

Maffesoli, Michel. *Time of the Tribes: The Decline of Individualism in Mass Society*. London: Sage, 1986.

Mathijs, Ernest. "Time Wasted." *FlowTV*, March 29, 2010. https://www.flowjournal.org/2010/03/time-wasted-ernest-mathijs-the-university-of-british-columbia/.

Mathijs, Ernest, and Jamie Sexton. *Cult Cinema: An Introduction*. Chichester, UK: Wiley-Blackwell, 2011.

McCulloch, Richard. "'Most People Bring Their Own Spoons': *The Room*'s Participatory Audiences as Comedy Mediators." *Participations* 8, no. 2 (November 2011): 189–218.

Meisner, Sandford, and Dennis Longwell. *Sanford Meisner on Acting*. New York: Random House, 1987.

Middlemost, Renee. "Renovating *The Room*: Audience Reception and Paratextual Intervention." *Celebrity Studies* 10, no. 2 (2018): 247–64. https://doi.org/10.1080/19392397.2018.1492429.

Mittell, Jason. *Complex TV: The Poetics of Contemporary Television Storytelling*. New York: NYU Press, 2015.

Modleski, Tania. *The Women Who Knew Too Much: Hitchcock and Feminist Theory*. London: Methuen, 1988.

Montgomery, Robert Shawn. "Cryptokubrology." Zero Zero Two. Accessed June 26, 2010. http://www.zerozerotwo.org/KUBRICK/KUBROLOGY/MAZEgate.html.

Nancy, Jean-Luc. *The Inoperative Community*. London: Sage, 1988.

Newman, Michael Z. *Indie: An American Film Culture*. New York: Columbia University Press, 2011.

Nietzsche, Friedrich. *On the Genealogy of Morality*. Edited by Keith Ansell-Pearson. Translated by Carol Diethe. New York: Cambridge University Press, 2006.

Palmer, Landon. "The American Dream of Middle Aged White Guys Making Bad Movies." *Film School Rejects*, October 14, 2014. https://filmschoolrejects.com/the-american-dream-of-middle-aged-white-guys-making-bad-movies-97e8149265e1/.

———. "Culture Warrior: Making Sense of *The Room*." *Film School Rejects*, October 12, 2010. https://filmschoolrejects.com/culture-warrior-making-sense-of-the-room-57537b46b99a/.

———. "6 Filmmaking Tips from Tommy Wiseau." *Film School Rejects*, January 8, 2014. https://filmschoolrejects.com/6-filmmaking-tips-from-tommy-wiseau-50563905e589/.

Parry, Judge. *Don Quixote of the Mancha*. Illustration by Walter Crane. New York: John Lane Company, 1919. https://www.gutenberg.org/files/55106/55106-h/55106-h.htm#Illus03.

Pavlounis, Dimitrios. "Sincerely Celebrating Failure: Tommy Wiseau's *The Room* and the Search for Sincerity." *Spectator: University of Southern California Journal of Film & Television* 32 (2012): 24–30. https://cinema.usc.edu/archivedassets/32_1/4_Pavlounis.pdf.

Poniewozik, James. "All-TIME 100 TV Shows." *TIME*, August 13, 2007. https://entertainment.time.com/2007/09/06/the-100-best-tv-shows-of-all-time/slide/mystery-science-theater-3000/.

Priambodho, H. S. "'The Mother of All Bad Movies': An Audience Research on the Culture of Tommy Wiseau's *The Room* Based on the Live Cinematic Experience." In *Excellent MSc Dissertations 2018*, edited by D. N. Duru, 169–202. Lund, Sweden: Lund University, 2018.

Ritman, Alex. "The Story behind Tommy Wiseau's Secret *Disaster Artist* Cameo (One for Which He Wants a SAG Campaign)." *Hollywood Reporter*, December 4, 2017. https://www.hollywoodreporter.com/news/story-behind-tommy-wiseau-s-secret-disaster-artist-cameo-one-he-wants-a-sag-campaign-1062510.

RockHaven Pictures/Rick Harper. "This Is Why You Haven't Seen *Room Full of Spoons* . . . Yet." Kickstarter Backer Update 14. June 6, 2016. https://www.kickstarter.com/projects/579574455/room-full-of-spoons-the-documentary-about-the-room/posts/1596350.

Rodkey, Christopher. "*God's Not Dead* as Reverse Revenge Fantasy." *An und für sich* (blog). April 2, 2016. https://itself.blog/2016/04/02/gods-not-dead-as-reverse-revenge-fantasy/.

Rose, Steve. "Is This the Worst Movie Ever Made?" *Guardian*, September 9, 2009. https://www.theguardian.com/film/filmblog/2009/sep/10/cinema-the-room-cult.

Rosen, Adam. "Should Gloriously Terrible Movies like *The Room* Be Considered 'Outsider Art'?" *Atlantic*, October 8, 2013. https://www.theatlantic.com/entertainment/archive/2013/10/should-gloriously-terrible-movies-like-em-the-room-em-be-considered-outsider-art/280393/.

Ross, Andrew. *No Respect: Intellectuals and Popular Culture*. New York: Routledge, 1989.

Rothfeld, Becca. "Sanctimony Literature." *Liberties Journal* 1, no. 3.

Sarris, Andrew. "Notes on the Auteur Theory in 1962." *Film Culture* 27, no. 27 (Winter 1962/1963): 1–8.

Schaefer, Eric. *"Bold! Daring! Shocking! True!": A History of Exploitation Films, 1919–1959*. Durham, NC: Duke University Press, 1999.

Sconce, Jeffrey. "Esper, the Renunciator: Teaching 'Bad' Movies to Good Students." In *Defining Cult Films: The Cultural Politics of Oppositional Taste*, edited by Mark Jancovich, Antonio Lazaro Reboll, Julian Stringer, and Andy Willis, 14–34. Manchester: Manchester University Press, 2003.

Sestero, Greg, and Tom Bissell. *The Disaster Artist: My Life inside The Room, the Greatest Bad Movie Ever Made*. New York: Simon and Schuster, 2013.

Sontag, Susan. "Notes on 'Camp.'" In *Against Interpretation and other Essays*, 277–93. New York: Dell, 1966.

Thornton, Sarah. *Club Cultures: Music, Media and Subcultural Capital*. Oxford: Polity Press, 1995.

Truffaut, François. "A Certain Tendency in French Cinema." In *Movies and Methods: An Anthology*, edited by Bill Nichols, 221–37. Berkeley, CA: University of California Press, 1976.

Wiseau, Tommy. "Interview with Tommy Wiseau." *The Room*, special ed. DVD. Directed by Tommy Wiseau. Los Angeles: Wiseau-Films, 2005.

Wolfe, Tom. *The Painted Word*. New York: Penguin, 1975.

Wood, Robin. *Hitchcock's Films Revisited*. London: Faber and Faber, 1989.

INDEX

Note: Page numbers in *italics* refer to illustrations.